W9-BOH-148

Naughty Needles

SEXY, SAUCY KNITS

FOR THE BEDROOM
AND BEYOND

Naughty Needles

SEXY, SAUCY KNITS
FOR THE BEDROOM AND BEYOND

NIKOL LOHR

PHOTOGRAPHY BY ROBYN EDEN
ILLUSTRATIONS BY RON MILLER

POTTER CRAFT

NEW YORK

Copyright © 2006 by Nikol Lohr

All rights reserved.

Published in the United States by Potter Craft,

an imprint of the Crown Publishing Group,

a division of Random House, Inc., New York.

www.crownpublishing.com

www.pottercraft.com

POTTER CRAFT and CLARKSON N. POTTER

are trademarks, and POTTER and colophon are

registered trademarks of Random House, Inc.

Library of Congress Cataloging-in-Publication Data

Lohr, Nikol.
Naughty needles : sexy, saucy knits for the bedroom and beyond / Nikol Lohr; photographs by Robyn Eden.
p. cm.
ISBN-13: 978-0-307-33737-5 (pbk.)
ISBN-10: 0-307-33737-5 (pbk.)
1. Knitting—Patterns. I. Title.
TT820.L75 2006
746.43'2041—dc22
2006023379

ISBN-13: 978-0-307-33737-5

ISBN-10: 0-307-33737-5

Printed in China

Design by Natalie Slocum

Photography by Robyn Eden

10 9 8 7 6 5 4 3 2 1

First Edition

For Ken & Kristi, who gave me creative genes
and for Ron, who inspires me and keeps me naughty

Thankyouthankyouthankyou

Supersized thanks to LB Deyo—without his help and direction, this book would still be just an idea—and to Kelly Sue DeConnick, who got me knitting in the first place.

Doubleplus thanks to my fabulous photographer and friend Robyn Eden, who's patient and thoughtful, and has always captured just what I had in mind. And to Ron Miller, for his inspired ideas, honest feedback, fetching illustrations, and for cheerfully enduring my hysteria and shamefully poor hygiene around deadlines.

Special thanks to Suzanne Link and Jay Mahavier for their endless hospitality. Sue, Kelly Sue, and Rebecca Gonzales also saved my life with all kinds of odds and ends, keeping me marginally sane during the photo shoots, which would liked to have killed me.

Wild thanks to all the amazing women who knitted their asses off for me and helped whip my patterns into submission: Adrian of Hello Yarn and Amber, Ann, Beth, Carolyn, Danielle, Jane, Janet, Jennifer, Jessica, Kelly Sue, Marissa, Rebecca, and Sarah of Maisy Day Handspun. And thanks to all the DH ladies, whose rousing discussion inspired the Baby Blue Ball Gag and, by extension, this whole book.

Equally wild thanks to my stunning models, who brought *Naughty Needles* to life: Amie, Amy, Angie, Brian, Chris Black, Christina, Curt, Gina, Jay, Jennifer, Johna, Katy, Kelly Sue, Kristi, Kristin, Laurenn, Leslie, Lester, Marian, Meghan, Michele, Michelle, Nancy, Nora Jean, Nathan, Rachel, Rebecca, Rita, Robyn, Ron, Ruby, Rushmi, Sandy, Suzanne, and Taylor. Whew!

Thanks so very, very much to editors Rosy Ngo and Christina Schoen at Potter Craft, for nurturing and disciplining *Naughty Needles*, and to art director Lauren Monchik, also at Potter Craft, for making her so damn pretty. My heart just swells at how crazyfuckingadorable this book is. Thanks also to Daniel Greenberg, my literary agent, for hooking me up with such a dandy imprint, and for being a marvelous problem solver. Thanks to Laurenn McCubbin for helping with the final images.

Thanks to the Longbranch Inn and Prototype, plus Rachel, Leslie, and Sue, for locations; to Mardy for the fancy chair; to Bell Wildlife Specialties of Harveyville, Kansas, for the wild animal skins; and to Toys in Babeland, for the Dirty Secrets goodies.

And finally, big fluffy heaps of thanks to my mom and dad, Kristi and Ken Lohr, who insisted that I was brilliant, and that I could do anything.

CONTENTS

INTRODUCTION

Knitting is Sexy

Knitting is sexy. There, I said it. If you're knitting plain wool socks or a grandma afghan, it doesn't matter—it's sexy. (Okay, maybe not Viggo Mortensen in *A History of Violence* sexy—more like Jon Stewart with an ass-kicking zinger.) Merging ingenuity and skill, taking ho-hum raw materials and bending them to your will to produce something entirely your own, something that works—whether aesthetically or practically—well, that's always hot. That's why chefs and mechanics alike make ladies swoon and men grumble (or swoon themselves, depending).

Knitting (or painting or writing code or building furniture) is sexy because it fuses vision and skill into a creative superpower. Doing something resourceful and productive feels like magic because it *is*. I mean, we're all basically the same. We all eat and sleep and hump and find things to fill the time in between. When you fill that time learning or perfecting something that not everyone can do, instead of just trudging to work or watching TV, you start to accumulate creative superpowers—and with them, a boost up on the human sexiness scale.

Factor in the wicked-looking implements that somehow create such soft and supple things, and knitting becomes doubly magical, doubly sexy.

So now that you've got this superpower, how's about using it for something a little more exciting than another scarf? (If you haven't ventured beyond scarves, don't fret. Most of these patterns are easy-peasy, and the few tougher techniques are detailed in the back of the book.)

Why *Naughty Needles?* It all started when my friend Kelly Sue gave me a copy of Debbie Stoller's *Stitch 'N Bitch*. I was immediately seduced by how damn cute knitting could be. But I was also intimidated. I was overtly crafty (sewing in preschool, crocheting in second grade), but knitting just looked so . . . sophisticated and mysterious—like chess next to tick-tack-toe.

When I finally sat down with needles and yarn, everything changed. Within an hour, I had religion. Unfortunately, I also had trouble finding patterns that fit my aesthetic but tolerated my limited skill set, budget, and attention span. Winging it was out of the question. Unlike freeform crochet, which lets you see what you've got as you progress, freeform knitting often won't reveal its true size or shape until it's almost done—and by then, it's too late. And while I do enjoy the exhilaration of ripping back hours' worth of work in a few short moments as much as the next gal, I'm not so keen on the wasted time and ravaged yarn.

I quickly learned that skimpy, silly garments were just the ticket: Quick, gratifying, less heart-breaking to rip out, and amusing to explain. When the old man on the bus asks what you're making and you get to answer "vibrator cozy," it makes knitting that much more fun. So between camo skull halter top triumphs (jury duty) and sparkle fur bikini failures (sad hospital visits), I quietly toyed with a notion I'd had a few years earlier.

I'd been interviewed for what I was told would be an article about the resurgence in crafting. Instead, it was an indictment of traditional "wifely arts"—cooking, cleaning, crafting—as an insidious threat to The One True Feminism (an argument that just enrages me). I got all up in arms about being mislead and misinterpreted and, in my typical fashion of concocting elaborate, juvenile, and seldom-executed outlets for my indignation, I decided I'd crochet the author a sweet little baby blue ball gag to stuff in her big fat mouth. Then I thought, *Hmm, wait a minute, maybe there's something to that . . .*

And so *Naughty Needles* was born. (You'll get a knitted version of that ball gag in Chapter 4.) And while it's certainly brimming with eye candy, it's also chockablock with sexy, simple patterns, from sweet to spicy to a little silly. So whether you're dainty, daring, or downright dirty, bust out the needles and get ready to knit naughty.

About the Patterns

GAUGE

You've heard it before and you'll hear it again: don't neglect your gauge! Always make that swatch, and measure it over 4"/10cm instead of using that tempting little 2"/5cm window in your knitting gauge. (Why don't those have 4" windows? There's always room for a big window, but instead they stick you with that little 2" slot. It's infuriating!) I hosted a dozen knitting friends of all skill levels to test out my patterns, and I was amazed at how much gauge varied from knitter to knitter (generally, the slower knitters were a bit tighter and the breakneck knitters were seriously loose). A big difference in tension could ruin your garment and make you curse my name until your dying day. I'd rather avoid that, so knit your gorram swatch. If you need further motivation, you'll find general and pattern-specific uses for swatches at naughtyneedlesknitting.com. 🌐

I've specified the stitch for all swatches. In most cases, swatches are given in the dominant pattern stitch. I know some die-hards insist swatches should always be stockinette stitch, but there's so much variation in how people throw yarn while knitting in pattern that I feel a pattern gauge is safer.

SKILL LEVEL

If you know the basics (knitting, purling, binding off, seaming, etc.), you'll be set. The patterns range from easy-peasy to intermediate. There are a few intimidating techniques that a beginning knitter might not know, but I've explained them in simple, photographed steps in the "Techniques" section at the end (see p. 130). Remember, I'm a new knitter, too. If I can swing it, so can you. You should own a good reference, though, just in case. *Vogue Knitting Quick Reference* is extensive, slender, and highly portable.

SUPPLIES

Just as I assume you can knit, I also assume you have the basic materials required for every project: scissors, yarn needles, and a measuring tape or ruler so those won't be listed with every pattern. Project notions (fasteners) will be listed under "Yarn, etc.," while knitting notions (needles, stitch markers) will fall under "Needles & Notions."

YARN

All yarns were in production at the time of writing, but yarn companies constantly drop old lines or colors and introduce new ones. If a particular yarn has been discontinued or your LYS (local yarn store) doesn't carry it, then don't despair. Check naughtyneedlesknitting.com for a list of sources and substitutes, as well as notes and scans of swatches, so you can compare.

SIZING

Sizing is based on Yarn Council standards. In normal human terms, that translates to the average retail sizing with which you're probably accustomed. Small fits petite, slender, or small-breasted women—it's roughly women's size 4–6. Medium fits a slightly larger frame with a few curves: about a size 8. Large fits curvier or taller gals (10–12), and XL will be right for bigger or bustier gals (14–16). For the most part, these clothes are designed to fit closely, so garment dimensions will often be smaller than your actual measurements.

VARIATIONS

Many of the sexier and sillier patterns offer variation ideas to take them out of the bedroom. Check the sidebars for additional style and fiber ideas, pattern adaptations for chaster (or even naughtier) versions, and inspiration for your own custom creations. Don't be afraid to experiment. What's the worst thing that could happen? You waste a little time and a little yarn. Odds are the yarn costs less than seeing a bad movie—and you can probably salvage the yarn, unlike those two hours *Daredevil* robbed from you.

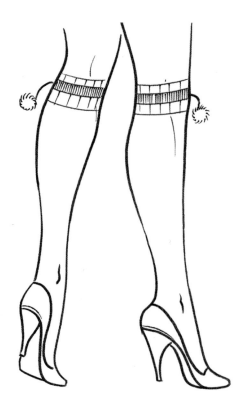

Bonuses

WEB EXTRAS

You'll also see little icons peppered here and there. A WEB icon means hit naughtyneedlesknitting.com for bonus patterns and variations we couldn't include here. The supporting site features even more ideas for varying and personalizing these patterns. You'll also find alternate yarn suggestions, swatches, links to resources and shops, a project gallery, and profiles of the wonderful knitters and models who helped with all the gorgeous little numbers in the book, along with corrections, tips, and suggestions from other knitters.

STASHBUSTER/SPEED QUEEN

Other items are marked STASHBUSTER or SPEED QUEEN. Those patterns accommodate a wide range of yarns (so you can cull your stash) or knit up in two to four hours or less, respectively.

Sugar and Spice and Everything Nice

preteens tarting themselves up like tiny hookers, overt sexiness has become almost creepy.

Maybe squeaky clean is the new dirty.

And happily, cutie-pie sexy (unlike vamp sexy) is a cinch to pull off on a daily basis. You're taking a risk as a Ginger, and everybody knows it. But if you fall on your face as a Mary Ann, you're still adorable (and no one's the wiser).

If you're a smidge too sullen or bitchy for Mary Ann, meet Der Kinderwhore (AKA Lolita, Jailbait, Catholic Schoolgirl). Anybody can rock the Kinderwhore look. That's why the old pigtails-and-knee-socks chestnut has such staying power. Whether you're chubby or skinny as a rail, busty or flat chested, Amazon tall or pixie small, goth or junior league, president of the math club or smokin' in the girls' room: the look works. And unlike the other sex-costume classics (Naughty Nurse, French Maid, Slutty Cheerleader), a well-crafted Kinderwhore outfit will pass as actual clothing, so you get the illusion of indifference. And there's nothing sexier than being sexy accidentally.

Sadly, however, there is a cutoff point for Kinderwhore. When you're of a certain age, it's best to transition from Naughty Schoolgirl to Naughty Librarian, Naughty Secretary, or Naughty House-wife. Otherwise, one terrible day, you'll shoot for Lolita and wind up as Baby Jane.

B Y SECOND GRADE, I knew with satisfying certainty that as a grown woman, instead of slouching into a flannel housecoat and terry cloth scuffs at the end of the day, I would slink into my feathery babydoll nightie and matching marabou-puff high heels. It was the perfect sleepwear for my terribly exciting and impressive future career: secret agent/veterinarian/movie star/ reporter. Maybe the American sex kitten cliché wasn't the wisest foundation on which to build my dazzling future life, but in a world of potluck suppers and coloring books and after-school snacks, a life that included impractical underwear was an exotic life indeed.

I may not always live up to my childhood expectations of everyday glamour, but what rated as sexy when I was a little girl is just as compelling to me today. My girlhood feminine idols were '70s television icons: Charlie's Angels, Nancy Drew, Diana Prince (*Wonder Woman*), Isis, Samantha (*Bewitched*), and Jeannie (*I Dream of Jeannie*). That same nostalgic, fresh-scrubbed television sexiness inspires this first chapter. These seven patterns are mostly Mary Ann, with a little Lolita, and just a pinch of Ginger. Nothing in this chapter would make your mom flustered—at least not at first blush.

And while the fluttery eyelashes and lip gloss and pink chiffon of it all is a little corny, there's something both comforting and surprisingly titil-lating about the aesthetic. After all, with today's

. . . In a world of potlucks and coloring books, a life that included impractical under-wear was an exotic life indeed.

Fembot

Based on classic Hollywood-style nighties sold by mail order in mid-century women's magazines, this babydoll is knit with a mix of lace and novelty yarns to mimic feathers and chiffon. The blend of two different eyelash lengths and textures, or the use of a multitextured combination yarn, is essential for a rich, feathery look. The *Austin Powers* Fembots lent a tinge of wickedness to the classic ultra-femme pastel version, but if the wide-eyed girlishness of all that pink still turns your gut, knit the black version for a Samantha/Serena naughty doppelganger vibe with all the retro appeal but none of the priss. Rowwr!

SIZING
Women's S (M, L, XL)

Where no parentheses are used, instructions/quantities apply to all sizes

YARN
For pink and white Fembot:
1 (1, 2, 2) balls Crystal Palace *Kid Merino* (25g; 240yd/220m; 44% nylon, 28% kid mohair, 28% merino wool), 4669 blush (A)

1 (1, 2, 2) balls Lion Brand *Fun Fur* (50g; 64yd/58m; 100% polyester), 100 white (B)

1 (1, 2, 2) balls Bernat *Boa* (50g; 71yd/65m; 100% polyester), 81005 dove (C)

1 ball Cascade *Fixation* (50g; 100yd/91m; 98.3% cotton, 1.7% elastic), 3077 pale pink (D)

For black Fembot:
1 (1, 2, 2) balls Karabella *Gossamer* (50g; 222yd/203m; 30% kid mohair, 52% nylon, 18% polyester), 6700 black with black (A)

1 (1, 2, 2) balls Moda Dea *Prima* (50g; 72yd/66m; 51% nylon, 49% polyester), 3012 black (B)

1 ball Cascade *Fixation* (50g; 100yd/91m; 98.3% cotton, 1.7% elastic), 8990 black (D)

Note: For the black version, there is no C yarn.

NEEDLES & NOTIONS
US 3/3.25mm circular needles (24"/61cm max, shorter is easier), or for gauge

US 11/8mm circular needles (24"/61cm max, shorter is easier), or for gauge

US 3/3.25mm or other small size double-pointed needles, preferably metal (or use smallest circular)

Stitch markers

Small safety pins or locking stitch markers

GAUGE
ALWAYS CHECK YOUR GAUGE! Measure unwashed and unblocked, relaxed and patted flat NOT smoothed out.

[1] Stockinette st, A+B(+C) together on larger needles: 12 sts = 4"/10cm

[2] K1, P1 rib, A+D together on smaller needles: pink: 25 sts = 4"/10cm; black: 21 sts = 4"/10cm

INSTRUCTIONS

CUP

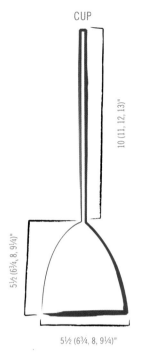

10 (11, 12, 13)"

5½ (6¾, 8, 9¼)"

5½ (6¾, 8, 9¼)"

CUPS

Use A, B (and C in the pink) held together to knit the cups, then drop all but A and change needle size for the straps. Maintain a smooth edge by slipping the first and knitting the last stitch of every row.

With A, B (and C) held tog and larger needles, CO 8 (10, 12, 14) sts, PM, CO 8 (10, 12, 14) sts.

Rows 1–13 (13, 15, 15): Work in stockinette st, slipping first and knitting last sts on all rows.

Row 14 (14, 16, 16): Sl 1, p to within 3 st from marker, p2tog, p1, SM, p1, ssp, p to last st, k1—14 (18, 22, 26) sts.

K next row (RS).

Continue as above, decreasing one st on either side of marker on every purled row until you have 10 sts.

Work 1 RS row.

Next WS row: Sl 1, (p2tog) twice, SM, (ssp) twice, k1—6sts.

Next 2 rows: Drop B (and C). Switch to dpns and start your I-cord.

K I-cord for 10 (11, 12, 13)"/25 (28, 30, 33)cm, transfer stitches to safety pin and break yarn, leaving 24"/61cm tail.

SKIRT

Make a ribbed band with A and D, drop D and change to larger needles for the sheer part, then add B (and C) for the furry hem.

Pink version:

Using D and smaller circular needles, CO 124 (134, 144, 154) sts. With long-tail cast-on, join, being careful not to twist.

Both the straps and the skirt will look too short when you knit them, but they'll stretch a good deal from the weight of the garment/hemline.

Black version:

Using D and smaller circular needles, CO 104 (114, 124, 134) sts with long-tail CO. Join, being careful not to twist sts.

Both versions:

PM. Add A. Work 3 (3, 5, 5) rnds k1, p1 rib.

Round 4: Drop D, switch to larger needles. K every rnd.

After 3"/8cm (measured flat): Inc 1 st every 10th st for 1 rnd. Don't worry about the leftover sts.

Knit 3"/8cm. Inc 1st every 11th st for 1 rnd.

Knit 3"/8cm. Inc 1st every 12th st for 1 rnd.

If necessary, knit until stockinette portion measures 9 (9, 9½, 10)"/23 (23, 24, 25)cm (measured flat, not hanging).

Add B (and C on pink version).

P 3 rnds (or more if you like).

FINISHING

Use safety pins to mark sides and center front and back.

Pin cups to chest band with 4 pins spaced evenly. Using additional safety pins, attach straps flush with band 2"/5cm from either side of center back marker.

Try on nightie to check strap length and cup position. Adjust cups as necessary and sew into place using A. Knit or pull out rows as necessary for correct strap length, then bind off and sew to band 2"/5cm from either side of center back marker. Remove all pins and weave in ends.

SKIRT

Flat: 10 (10¾, 11½, 12½)"

9 (9, 9½, 10)"

Variations

Skip the cups for a sexy see-through version. (Complete pattern online.)

Omit the cups and straps for a sexy evening capelet.

Make the larger sizes of the luxe black version more economical by substituting an inexpensive plain black mohair such as Plymouth Le Fibre Nobili *Imperiale* (25g; 109yd/100m; 80% super kid mohair, 20% nylon) for every other row of Karabella *Gossamer* in the cups and hemline. You'll get away with just one ball of the luxury *Gossamer* without compromising the glitz.

For more modest, ass-concealing lines, knit 2–3"/5-8cm more in A before starting the hemline trim. Adjust yarn requirements accordingly.

For more control, slip 12"/30cm of sheer ribbon through the bottom center edge stitches on either cup, then tie in a bow to adjust cup positioning.

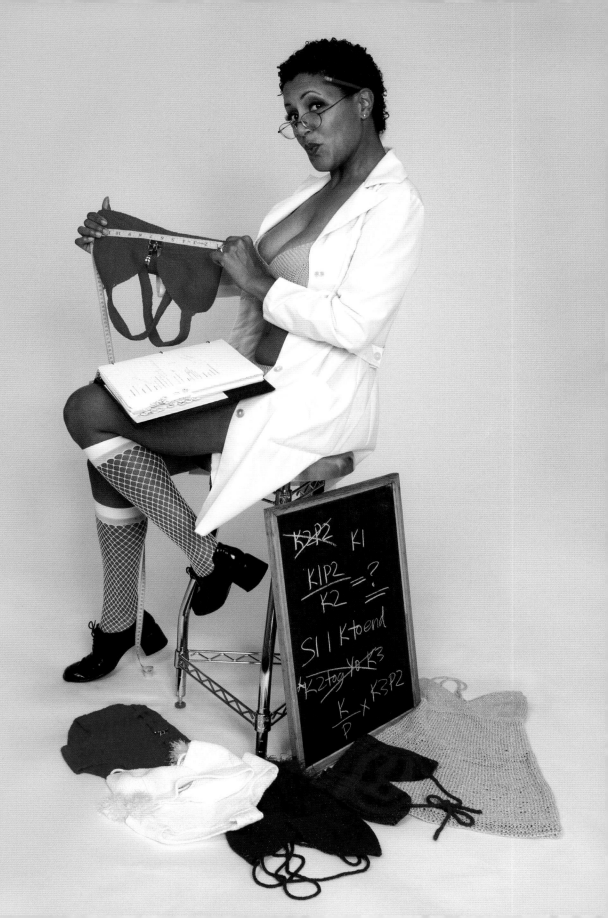

The Great Bikini Experiment

SIZING
Women's S (M, L, XL)

NEEDLES, GAUGE, YARN
See each variation

A lightly tailored top and a basic bikini bottom form the frame-work of these three divergent variations. In fact, this family of garments is really a study in pattern modification geared to get you thinking of ways to personalize any pattern to suit your taste and style. Although the instructions are essentially the same, the yarn choices and a few simple changes take them from bedside to beachside, dawn to dusk. As an added bonus: Once you've knit one, the others will be cake.

The basic pattern is built on two gently shaped cups, a band of varying thickness, and two straps. The right cup is knit in garter and turned opposite side out and the left cup is purled in reverse garter. If you hate purling, work the second cup first. If you really hate purling, you can knit them both, but the dart seams will look a bit different.

For the basic bottoms, these little cuties sport that ironic '70s styling—they're full-cut and modest under your ass and around your legs to keep them from riding up your butt, but low enough at the waistline to threaten to reveal ass cleavage. Saucy! (Of course, your ass-cleavage risk correlates directly with the size of your ass. Me, I'm in constant peril.)

The bottoms are knit flat in garter stitch, all in one piece, then joined at the sides with a garter mattress stitch. Along the legs (but not along the sides, where they'll be seamed), slip the first stitch of every row. This will form a nice, finished chain edge along your legs—or give you a clean surface for crocheting or knitting up trim, should you so choose.

INSTRUCTIONS

Basic Top

RIGHT CUP

Note: You'll slip the first and knit the last stitch of every row (on the knit rows, this will take care of itself). This forms a neat chain stitch along either side, with one link for every two rows. You'll always decrease at the start of even rows. If you lose your bearings, look for the tail: Knit towards it on even rows and away on odd rows.

With larger needles (medium needles for Bond Girl variation), CO 24 (30, 36, 42) sts.

Rows 1–5: Sl 1, k to end.

Row 6: Sl 1, k2tog, k to end.

Rows 7–11: Sl 1, k to end.

Row 12: Sl 1, k2tog, k to end.

Continuing: Decrease in the same way at the beginning of every **4th** row until you have 16 (20, 24, 28) sts.

FORM DART

Without turning work, and continuing to hold the yarn with your usual hand, pick up and knit *through both sides* of each of the chain sts you've formed down the straight (non-decrease) edge. At first, this is going to leave you with a pretty tight, awkward row on your needle. But as you knit away from the turn, it will loosen up and knit more easily.

TAPER SIDE AND BACK

Continue to decrease at the beginning of every 4th row until you have 24 (30, 36, 42) sts on your needle.

Then, decrease every other row until you're out of sts. You've made your first cup! Isn't it cute? Try it on!

LEFT CUP

CO 24 (30, 36, 42) sts.

Rows 1–5: Sl 1, p to 1 st from end, k1.

Row 6: Sl 1, p2tog, p to 1 st from end, k1.

Rows 7–11: Sl 1, p to 1 st from end, k1.

Row 12: Sl 1, p2tog, p to 1 st from end, k1.

Decrease in this way at the beginning of every 4th row, and always knitting the last st, until you have 16 (20, 24, 28) sts.

FORM DART

Without turning work, pick up and knit sts in *just the far side* of each of the chain sts you've formed along the straight (non-decreased) edge.

Continue decreasing at the beginning of every 4th row until you have 24 (30, 36, 42) sts on your needle.

Then, decrease every other row until you're out of sts.

BAND

If you're struggling to pick up stitches, first make sure you're still holding the yarn with your usual hand (switching hands is a common mistake and makes picking up stitches difficult). If that's not the problem, try using both needles. Just slide the left needle into the stitch you're picking up into to hold it open. Then, with the right needle, proceed exactly as if knitting the stitch normally. In tight spaces, use a smaller needle on the left.

When working the band, the center stitches after the dart will be tighter and a little harder to pick up than the chain stitches along the sides of the cup, and those overlapped stitches are really a bitch. You can use a US 1 or 2/2.5mm or 2.75mm needle in your left hand to open up the stitches and guide your working needle through.

EDGE STITCHES

Slipping the first stitch of each row in combination with knitting the last stitch of every row gives you a tidy chain link for every 2 rows. This makes it east to knit down one edge to form the bust dart and forms a smooth, decorative stitch on the other edge.

If you're unfamiliar with a slipped-stitch edge, here how it works: Looking at the row you're about to knit, and with the yarn in front (as it would be if you were purling), slip the 1st stich from your left need to your right needle, purlwise (inserting the right needle into the stitch from the right). Move the yarn to the back if necessary (i.e., if you're about ot knit), and proceed as directed for the row. For the edge to work, the last stitch of every row also needs to be knit, so if you're purling a row, don't forget to knit that final stitch.

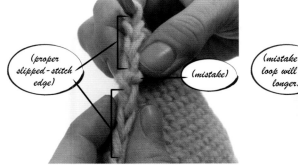
(proper slipped-stitch edge) (mistake)

(mistake—loop will be longer)

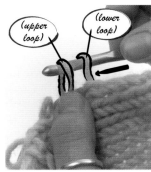
(upper loop) (lower loop)

Pay attention as you knit. It's easy to forget and knit the first stitch instead of slipping it, which created a knot like this is the middle of your pretty edge.

If you botch the nondecreasing side (which forms the dart and the bottom edge of the cup), you can blow it off, since you'll be picking up and knitting into it anyway.

To correct, just drop the last stitch on the row and unravel each edge chain until you've undone the offending stitch.

Using a crochet hook, draw each stich through the one below it, as if to fixing a dropped stockinette stitch in the middle of the row—only it's way easier, because they're big, roomy loops.

21

Count in 7 (8, 9, 10) sts from the center of each cup. Overlap and pin.

Tie the loose threads at each tapered back end together to keep it all straight and tight (you can always unknot them before you weave them in if that's your thing).

With RS facing, using smaller circular needles, and starting with the back side (narrower wedge) of right cup, pick up 1 st into each st along bottom edge until you hit the dart. Then pick up and knit 3 sts for every 4 presented, which draws it up just a bit. When you get to the overlap, be sure to pick up your sts through both layers. When you hit the other dart, go back to picking up every st.

When you've picked up all sts along the bottoms of both cups, then join: slip that first picked up st to the right needle, then pass the last picked-up st from the right (which is now the second st on your right needle) up and over the transferred st and onto the left needle. (So basically, those two end sts have just switched positions.) This will form a nice, snug join. Having those end threads knotted here keeps everything from getting slack.

Continue band as directed by variation instructions.

STRAPS

There's no such thing as universal tit placement, so let's not direct universal strap placement. Instead, try on the top and mark with pins or yarn where the straps look best. Here's how:

With one hand at the top edge of each cup, gently lift the cups from various points along the edge until you find your ideal strap position, then place a safety pin or marker at that spot. The best spot will look sexy, but if you hop around, it won't make you feel like your tits will pop at out any moment. (If you want, hop up and down in the mirror to check. It's funny.) Wider-set breasts will actually want closer straps, which seems counterintuitive, but prevents pop-outs.

Pick up and knit and/or affix straps as directed per each pattern, centering over marked spot.

WHY I LOVE FREDERICK'S

Since the '40s, the Frederick's of Hollywood catalog has championed playful bedroom clothes devised either to lure you into bed or to keep you there. Ostensibly offering a helping hand for happier marriages (with headlines like "Do it for him!"), Frederick's spread falsies, push-up bras, and crotchless panties from coast to coast through mail-order catalogs and ads in lowbrow women's (and men's) magazines.

In the '70s, Frederick's ditched its winsome, cheery illustrations in favor of photographs, and now the models are as enhanced, airbrushed, and blank-faced as Playmates. But while the modern Frederick's catalog may have lost much of its whimsy and delicious seediness, it will always beat out the uptown panty-hawkers in naughtiness and nostalgia. Frederick's can't be beat for those pinup-flavored, tasty but timeworn classic costumes that don't quite make sense on a snotty, joyless Victoria's Secret supermodel—but that are right at home in the American bedroom. Peekaboo babydolls, marabou slippers, "fantasy" costumes, crotchless panties, cupless bras, stripper shoes—all those dress-up clichés became clichés for a good reason. Hooray for Hollywood!

Basic Bottom

If you have generous proportions and/or ass cleavage enrages you and makes you want to shake your angry fist at the kids these days, you can sub the Gidget variation knit in straight garter stitch (with the taper, but no stitch changes for stripes, no belt) for grannier coverage. You'll need to add an extra ball of yarn (the coy Gidget adds a total of 48 more rows, the equivalent of almost a whole extra front panel).

Alternately, you can knit in several short rows (see "Techniques," p. 133) about 20 rows into the back panel for hip-hugging lines without plumber's butt.

FRONT

With larger needles, CO 72 (82, 92, 102) sts.

Knit 50 (54, 58, 62) rows in garter st.

Row 51 (55, 59, 63): BO 21 (23, 25, 27) sts, k to end.

Row 52 (56, 60, 64): BO 21 (23, 25, 27) sts, k to end.

TAPER LEG OPENINGS TO CROTCH

Along legs, always slip the first stitch purlwise!

Sl 1, k2tog, k to the last 3 sts, ssk, k1.

Next 2 rows: Sl 1, k to end.

Continue to dec every 3rd row as above until you have 18 (20, 22, 24) stitches.

CROTCH

Along crotch, continue to slip the first stitch of every row.

Knit 3 (3, 3½, 4)/7.5 (7.5, 9, 10)cm.

BACK REAR PANEL

SHAPE BOTTOM

Sl 1, M1, knit to last st, M1, k1.

Repeat last row until you have 64 (74, 84, 94) sts.

Then inc as above every other row until you have 80 (90, 100, 110) sts.

With WS facing (if you're on the RS, knit an extra row first), k 50 (54, 58, 62) rows in garter st.

FINISHING

Join sides with garter mattress st (if you're rusty, there's a dandy description on knitty.com). Weave in ends.

Not That Innocent

Cheerleaders, tennis socks, roller skate puff-balls, those tempting tail tufts of Playboy Bunny uniforms. Something about the fluffy wiggle and bounce of pom-poms is both mesmerizing and stimulating. Maybe it's a mutant genetic impulse, a confused modern evolutionary trigger. Heck, mating and subsequent parenthood itself may well be driven by the subconscious impulse to surround oneself with all those pom-pom-studded baby duds. Who knows?

Add to that theory too much wine, my favorite marabou hair poms, and a Britney Spears doll, and I got to wondering: Would festooning my underwear with pompoms make me the ultimate cutsiepoo sex magnet? Thus the Not That Innocent bralet and panties were born. They're knit of stretch cotton yarn for a soft matte finish and extra cling, with dangling fun fur pom-poms that create so much darn cuteness you could scream. If you want to go absolutely nuts, knit up a pair of matching Kinderwhore knee socks or Lolita sock garters and festoon those with pom-poms as well. And as long as you're crossing the line, you may as well make a couple extras ones for your ponytails.

Oops.

SIZING
Women's S (M, L, XL)

Where no parentheses are used, instructions/quantities apply to all sizes

YARN
3 (3, 4, 4) balls Cascade *Fixation* (50g; 100yd/91m; 98.3% cotton, 1.7% elastic), 8001 white (A)

1 ball Lion Brand *Fun Fur* (50g; 60yd/54m; 100% polyester), 101 soft pink (B)

NEEDLES & NOTIONS
US 5/3.75mm circular needles (24"/61cm max), or for gauge

US 3/3.25mm circular needles (24"/61cm max), or for gauge

US 3/3.25mm or other small size double pointed needles (or use smaller circular)

2"/5cm pom-pom maker

Stitch markers

Safety pins (or locking stitch markers)

GAUGE
ALWAYS CHECK YOUR GAUGE! Measure unwashed and unblocked, just relaxed and patted flat (NOT smoothed out)

Garter and reverse garter st (all purled), A on larger needles: 25½ sts = 4"/10cm

INSTRUCTIONS

You don't want to overstretch the elastic in this yarn while you knit, so keep the tension nice and loose. This will keep your knitting true and will prevent things from going terribly, terribly wrong should you drop a stitch. (On the other hand, if you maintain a loose tension, the elastic does a fine job of holding dropped stitches snug and steady, so pickups are actually easier than usual.)

Bralet

With larger needles and A, knit cups as directed for Basic Top.

Using smaller needles, pick up and knit and join cups as for Basic Top. Then PM and knit 25 rows in garter st (alternating between k and p rows, because you're knitting in the round) and BO loosely.

STRAPS

Mark place as directed in main pattern. Using A, pick up and knit 3 sts and knit 8"/20.5cm of I-cord. Transfer live sts to safety pins or locking stitch markers. Break yarn, leaving 36"/91.4cm tails.

Pin straps to back 3"/7.5cm from center. Try on for fit, then unravel or continue knitting to perfect length. BO and sew straps to back.

Panty

Knit Basic Bottom in A.

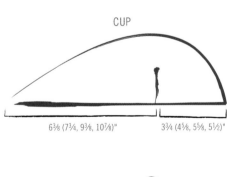

CUP

6⅜ (7¾, 9⅜, 10⅞)"   3¾ (4⅝, 5⅝, 5½)"

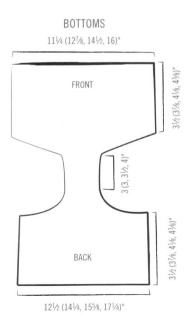

BOTTOMS

11¼ (12⅞, 14½, 16)"

FRONT

3½ (3⅞, 4⅛, 4⅜)"

3 (3, 3½, 4)"

BACK

3½ (3⅞, 4⅛, 4⅜)"

12½ (14¼, 15⅝, 17¼)"

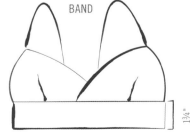

BAND

1¾"

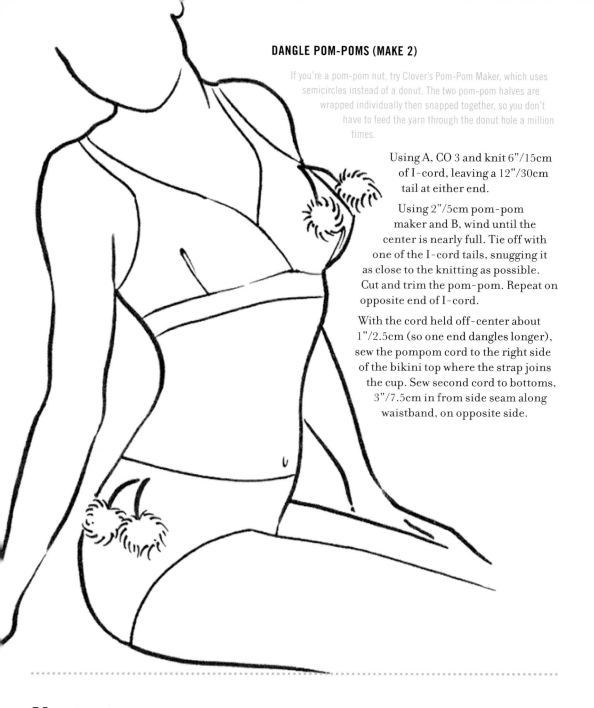

DANGLE POM-POMS (MAKE 2)

If you're a pom-pom nut, try Clover's Pom-Pom Maker, which uses semicircles instead of a donut. The two pom-pom halves are wrapped individually then snapped together, so you don't have to feed the yarn through the donut hole a million times.

Using A, CO 3 and knit 6"/15cm of I-cord, leaving a 12"/30cm tail at either end.

Using 2"/5cm pom-pom maker and B, wind until the center is nearly full. Tie off with one of the I-cord tails, snugging it as close to the knitting as possible. Cut and trim the pom-pom. Repeat on opposite end of I-cord.

With the cord held off-center about 1"/2.5cm (so one end dangles longer), sew the pompom cord to the right side of the bikini top where the strap joins the cup. Sew second cord to bottoms, 3"/7.5cm in from side seam along waistband, on opposite side.

Variations

Skip the pom-poms for a comfy swimsuit or yoga outfit.

For a more substantial halter top, you'll need an extra ball of yarn: Increase the band to 40 rows, and pick up and knit 7 sts instead of 3 for the straps. Knit in garter rather than I-cord, slipping each 1st st for a smooth edge.

Gidget Goes Hawaiian

Okay, there's nothing overtly Hawaiian about this bikini. You may as well call it Gidget Goes Californ-ian or Gidget Gone Wild—that is, if Gidget likes to get wasted and flash her tits (the buckled front makes it tempting!). But with wide criss-cross straps, a fetch-ing front-buckle closure, wedgie-proof lines, and a darling little belt, this stretchy bikini is as Gidget as can be. Form follows function, so the bra band is doubled for extra support and beachside security (use the doubled band as a casing for roll-proof 1¼"/3cm elastic for even greater support). Stretchy Katrina yarn has built-in memory, and the garter stitch texture forgives a not-so-teenage ass.

SIZING
Women's S (M, L, XL)

Where no parentheses are used, instruc-tions/quantities apply to all sizes

YARN, ETC.
4 (4, 5, 5) balls Patons *Katrina* (100g; 163yd/150m; 92% rayon, 8% polyester), 10707 cherry

2 interlocking 1"x1"/2.5cm x 2.5cm metal buckle sets

OPTIONAL (FOR EXTRA SUPPORT)
1½ yd/1.4m roll-proof 1½"/3.8cm elastic

Sewing thread to match yarn

NEEDLES & NOTIONS
US 5/3.75mm circular needles (24"/61cm max), or for gauge

US 3/3.25mm circular needles (24"/61cm max), or for gauge

OPTIONAL (FOR EXTRA SUPPORT)
Machine or sewing needle

Large safety pin

GAUGE
ALWAYS CHECK YOUR GAUGE! Measure unwashed and unblocked, just relaxed and patted flat (NOT smoothed out).

Garter and reverse garter st (all purled), on larger needles: 21½ sts = 4" (10cm)

INSTRUCTIONS

Bikini top

CUPS

Knit cups using larger needles, as for Basic Top.

BAND

In this version, you'll start and end the band in the center front instead of center back, to accommodate the front closure. Knit stripes into the band, then continue in stockinette stitch to form the casing for the optional elastic reinforcement.

If you don't want to fuss with elastic, but you want extra support, knit every other row of the band through the back loop for a firmer, denser fabric.

With smaller needles and a 10"/25.5cm tail, CO 3 sts, then, with the front center and the RS (smooth dart) of cup facing you, pick up 1 st for every 2 sts you encounter until you reach the dart. (Picking up fewer stitches in the center of the cups helps compensate for the lack of overlap, versus the basic pattern.)

After the dart, pick up 1 st for each edge st (1 edge st = 2 rows) until you reach the end.

Continuing with center back of other cup, pick up and knit sts in the same manner all the way across (1 st per chain to the dart, then every other st to the end), then CO 3 more sts.

Working flat and always knitting first and last 3 sts of all purl rows, K4 rows.

P3 rows.

K1 row.

P1 row.

K6 rows.

Continue in stockinette st until you have a section totaling 11 rows stockinette st.

Fold the band in half along those last 3 rows of garter st, forming a boxy fold comprised of a purl row on either side of the fold and a flat knit bottom.

CUP

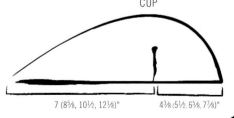

7 (8⅝, 10½, 12⅛)"   4⅜ (5½, 6⅝, 7⅞)"

CASING

To finish the band and form casing, slide your left needle under a previously knit stitch, then k2tog, using the live stitch and the false stitch you just lifted. After you've done this twice, you'll start binding off as well. So you'll be knitting the live edge down to the inside top of the band and binding the whole thing off at once. On the unattached little 3-stitch nubs that stick out on either side, you'll use the edge of the cast-on stitches; for the attached band, you'll use the top row of purl bumps. Since the rows go straight down without increase/decrease, you'll have exactly the same number of false stitches as you have live stitches, and it will finish beautifully.

If you're worried about which row to knit into, study the WS of your band where it connects to the cups. You'll knit that first row of purl bumps that looks nice and neat, directly under the picked-up edge. You don't want to knit into the picked-up edge itself for two reasons: 1) those extra stitches you ignored when you picked up the band will confuse you, and 2) that would produce a really bulky seam. This way, the seam flattens perfectly.

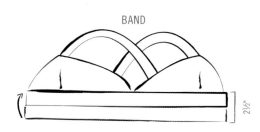

BAND

2½"

Holding the top with WS facing you and band folded over on itself, insert the left needle into the top of the first st of the little nub, k2tog, using both the st you lifted and the first live st on your needle.

Repeat for second st. BO 1.

Repeat to finish binding off nub.

Continue across entire band, using that top row of purl bumps (directly under the picked-up edge), as the sts you'll lift and knit together with the live st.

Try on the top before you add the buckles to get a sense of whether you want more support. If it feels fine, you can blow off the elastic. Otherwise, measure it to fit your ribs (you'll lose a bit sewing it down to the buckles, but the buckles themselves will make up the difference) and feed it through the casing, leading with a large safety pin. Sew down securely at either end.

FINISHING

Feed nub end through buckle loop, making sure buckle is facing the right way.

Whip-stitch end shut, then fold nub edge of band under, pulling snug so edge of buckle sits just inside center front edge of cup (band will stretch) and sewing down carefully with reserved tail.

Repeat on other side, being sure buckle faces the right way.

STRAPS (MAKE 2)

Knit every other row through the back loops for a firm strap. The straps will look short, but they stretch a good deal when on.

With smaller needles, CO 60 sts.

Row 1: Knit.

Row 2: Knit tbl.

Repeat Rows 1 & 2.

Row 5: Purl.

Row 6: Knit tbl.

Row 7: Knit.

Repeat Rows 6 & 7.

BO all sts.

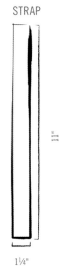

STRAP

11"

1¼"

FINISHING

Mark for placement, as in Basic Top, then seam straps centered at markers and criss-crossed in back, about 3"/7.6cm from center back.

Bottoms

These bottoms are taller than the Basic Bottom and taper a bit to the hip. They also have a knitted-in stockinette stripe pattern. You'll start with fewer stitches and inc 1 stitch with an M1 on each side every 4th row and knit in the stripe pattern at the same time until you achieve the CO number from Basic Bottom. Then proceed as usual and do the reverse on the back side.

PATTERNED UPPER EDGE (FRONT)

With larger needles, CO 60 (70, 80, 90) sts.

Rows 1–3: Knit row.

Row 4: K1, M1, k to 1 st from edge, M1, k1—62 (72, 82, 92) sts.

Rows 5–7: Knit.

Row 8: K1, M1, p to 1 st from edge, M1, k1—64 (74, 84, 94) sts.

Row 9: Knit.

Row 10: Purl.

Row 11: Knit.

Row 12: K1, M1, k to 1 st from edge, M1, k1—66 (76, 86, 96) sts.

Rows 13–15: Knit.

Row 16: K1, M1, k to 1 st from edge, M1, k1—68 (78, 88, 98) sts.

Row 17: Knit,

Row 18: Purl.

Row 19: Knit.

Row 20: K1, M1, k to 1 st from edge, M1, k1—70 (80, 90, 100) sts.

Row 21–23: Knit.

Row 24: K1, M1, k to 1 st from edge, M1, k1—72 (82, 92, 102) sts.

FRONT PANEL, CROTCH, AND BACK PANEL

Continue in garter st, starting with first row of Basic Bottom and continuing to end of Basic Bottom pattern, but don't BO yet.

PATTERNED UPPER EDGE (BACK)

Row 1: K1, k2tog, k to 3 sts from edge, ssk, k1—78 (88, 98, 108) sts.

Row 2–4: Knit.

Row 5: K1, k2tog, k to 3 sts from edge, ssk, k1—76 (86, 96, 106) sts.

Row 6: Knit.

Row 7: Purl.

Row 8: Knit.

Row 9: K1, k2tog, k to 3 sts from edge, ssk, k 1—74 (84, 94, 104) sts.

Rows 10–12: Knit.

Row 13: K1, k2tog, k to 3 sts from edge, ssk, k1—72 (82, 92, 102) sts.

Row 14: Knit.

Row 15: Purl.

Row 16: Knit.

Row 17: K1, p2tog, p to 3 from edge, ssp, k1—70 (80, 90, 100) sts.

Rows 18–20: Knit.

Row 21: K1, k2tog, k to 3 from edge, ssk, k1—68 (78, 88, 98) sts.

Rows 22–24: Knit.

BO all sts.

BELT

LEFT HALF

Using larger needles, CO 28 (33, 38, 43) sts.

Rows 1–3: Knit.

Row 4: K1, M1, p to 1 st from edge, k1—29 (34, 39, 44) sts.

Row 5: Knit.

Row 6: Purl.

Row 7: Knit.

Row 8: K1, M1, k to end—30 (35, 40, 45) sts.

Rows 9–11: Knit.

BO all sts.

RIGHT HALF

CO 28 (33, 38, 43) sts.

Rows 1–3: Knit.

Row 4: K1, p to 1 st from edge, M1, k1—29 (34, 39, 44) sts.

Row 5: Knit.

Row 6: Purl.

Row 7: Knit.

Row 8: K to 1 st from edge, M1, k1—30 (35, 40, 45) sts.

Rows 9–11: Knit.

Row 12: K to 1 st from edge, M1, k1—31 (36, 41, 46) sts.

BO all sts.

BOTTOMS
11 (13, 15, 17)"

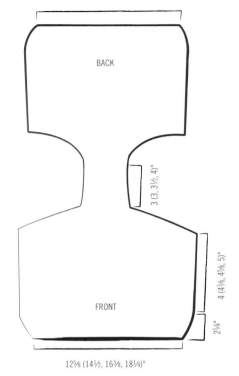

BACK

3 (3, 3½, 4)"

4 (4⅜, 4⅝, 5)"

FRONT

2¼"

12⅝ (14½, 16⅜, 18¼)"

BELT

1¼"

5⅝ (6½, 7⅜, 8⅜)"

BELT LOOPS

Place the belt loops at 2"/5cm and 4"/10cm from the front edges, one row down from edge.

Using larger needles and starting 1 row down from edge and 2"/5cm in from side seam, pick up and knit 4 sts.

K20 rows in garter st, slipping first st of each row.

Lay belt loop flat against bathing suit, then pick up and knit and BO into st directly below, as you did for top casing.

Repeat at 4"/10cm and at 2"/5cm and 4"/10cm from opposite side.

FINISHING

Position each belt half along the corresponding shaped edge, 4 rows down from top. Baste or pin edge of belt to edge of front.

Seam sides with garter mattress st, treating both the side sts and belt sts in the side seam as one side.

Loop free belt ends through buckle loops, then sew buckles to belt, making sure hardware is facing out. Weave in all ends.

Bond Girl

A metallic chain tube yarn, knit with different needle sizes, produces firm garter stitch cups and band for coverage and support and a fluid stockinette stitch midriff with a slinky drape. A sexy double strap adds a dash of elegance, and optional faux-fur trim completes the retro look. Dress it down with jeans or up with a velvet skirt or satin pants.

For a dress, simply continue increasing and knitting to desired length, and finish with a few rounds of garter (see variation notes). 🌐

Women's S (M, L, XL)

Where no parentheses are used,
instructions/quantities apply to all sizes

YARN
3 (3, 4, 4) Patons *Brilliant* (50g; 166yd/152m; 69% acrylic, 31% polyester), 04430 beautiful burgundy (A)

1 ball Moda Dea *Prima* (50g; 77yd/71m; 60% nylon, 40% polyester), 3377 burgundy (B) (optional, for trim)

NEEDLES & NOTIONS
US 3/3.25mm circular needles (24"/61cm max, shorter is easier), or for gauge

US 5/3.75mm circular needles (24"/61cm max, shorter is easier), or for gauge

US 11/8mm circular needles (24"/61cm max, shorter is easier), or for gauge

Stitch markers

Safety pins or locking stitch markers

Sewing needle and matching thread

GAUGE
ALWAYS CHECK YOUR GAUGE! Measure unwashed and unblocked, just relaxed and patted flat (NOT smoothed out)

[1] Garter st *and* reverse garter st (all purl), A on US 5/3.75mm needles: 23 sts = 4"/10cm

[2] Stockinette st, A on US 11/8mm needles: 14 sts = 4"/10cm

SUGAR AND SPICE AND EVERYTHING NICE

37

NAUGHTY NEEDLES

INSTRUCTIONS

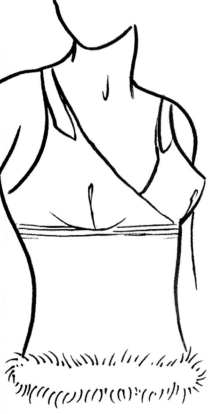

Use a sewing needle and single strand of matching thread to sew together yarn ends, overlapping 1"/2.5cm. This minimizes weaving ends on a yarn that tends to pop out.

CUPS

Using medium needles and A, knit cups as in Basic Top.

BAND AND MIDRIFF

Using smallest needles, pick up and join band as in Basic Top. PM.

Starting with a P rnd, alternate K and P rnds (circular garter st) for 7 (7, 9, 9) rnds, ending with a P rnd. For extra support, ktbl.

Switch back to medium needles. K1 rnd. P1 rnd.

Switch to large needles. *K2, k2tog, continue from * to end (knit any remainder sts).

Continue in stockinette (knitting all rnds) until you have 7½ (8, 8½, 9)"/19 (20, 22, 23)cm of stockinette st fabric (measure from below the garter portion).

Next row, add B and work both strands together (optional for trim). Alternate P and K rows to form garter st border. Work 5 rows, ending with a P row. BO LOOSELY.

STRAPS

Pick up and knit two skinny I-cord straps three rows from either side of marked spot (strap center).

Mark strap positioning as directed in Basic Top.

With RS facing you, using A and double-pointed needles, pick up and knit 2 sts, 3 rows toward center from strap marker. Tie off yarn end to secure, then knit 16"/40.5cm I-cord (lightly stretching to measure), noting the number of rows as you do, so your corresponding strap will match exactly. Break yarn, leaving 18"/45.5cm tail, and transfer live sts to safety pin or locking st marker.

With RS still facing, pick up and knit 2 sts, 3 rows towards garment side, away from strap marker. Tie off yarn end to secure, then knit 14"/35.5cm I-cord (lightly stretching to measure), again, noting number of rows. Break yarn, leaving 18"/46.5cm tail.

Repeat on opposite side, making the strap towards garment center the longer one and working the same number of rows, as noted on the first set of straps.

Pin all 4 straps to center back and try on garment. Unravel or knit on as necessary to achieve the perfect fit, making sure you unravel/knit the same number of rows on the two straps that correspond (two inner or two outer).

Starting with the 2 innermost straps, sew down to center back so that they touch at their close side. Sew down each of the 2 additional straps flush with their mates, so all 4 line up in a row. Weave in all ends.

Goldfinger Dress Variation

Inspired by Jill Masterson's glamorous, glittery corpse, this dress is simple, elegant, and shiny!

YARN
5 (5, 6, 7) balls Lion Brand *Glitter-spun* (50g; 115yd/105m; 60% acrylic, 27% cupro, 13% polyester), 990-170 gold

NEEDLES, NOTIONS & GAUGE
As for Bond Girl

INSTRUCTIONS

Proceed exactly as for Bond Girl, except:

After 6½"/16.5cm stockinette st on larger needles, increase every 5 sts for 1 rnd. Knit any remaining stitches.

Continue in stockinette st, repeating increase row every 6"/15cm.

Continue until stockinette st portion measures 19"/48.5cm (or to desired length). Work 5 rows in garter st (starting with P row), and BO LOOSELY.

Kinderwhore

If making fabric with sticks and string is magical, then socks are downright miraculous. Watching a three-dimensional shape emerge whole from your needles, as if by birth, is a joyous sight indeed. I finally understand why sock knitters have the creepy, hushed enthusiasm of Tori Amos fans.

If you've always been too intimidated by the scary jumble of double-pointed needles to try socks, you're in luck. This pair is knit using Cat Bordhi's excellent two-circular-needles method, so instead of managing a fistful of skewers in a precarious tangle of New Math, choking back the constant anxiety of dropping a needle, you'll use two circulars, switching back and forth between each pair and letting the other one hang slack. Circulars have the added benefit of allowing you safely try on your masterpiece while you knit for a perfect fit.

This extralong pair with a wide cuff features a snappy k2, p 1 rib knit on US 4/3.5mm needles to speed things up. They're knit in ultracuddly alpaca for unbelievable luxury and warmth (or try four balls of Knit Picks Merino Style if the alpaca breaks your bank).

SIZING
Women's one size

YARN
4 balls Blue Sky Alpacas *Sport Weight 100% Alpaca* (50g; 110yd/100m; 100% alpaca), 308 navy blue, or color of your choice (A)

1 ball Laines Du Nord *Giunco* (50g; 137yd/125m; 100% merino wool), 112 havy blue (or coordinating or contrasting color of choice)* (B)

*You can use about 30 yd/27m of sport or light worsted 100% wool from your stash instead.

NEEDLES & NOTIONS
2 US 4/3.5mm circular needles (16"/40.5cm or longer), or for gauge

Stitch markers

If at all possible, use Addi Turbo (metal), Addi Natura (bamboo), or Bryspun Flexible (plastic) circular needles. The flexible, lightweight cords will prevent fatigue and speed your knitting (the Denise needles are also light, but the smallest size is a 5—which might work if you're a tight knitter).

GAUGE
ALWAYS CHECK YOUR GAUGE!
Measure unwashed and unblocked, just relaxed and patted flat (NOT smoothed out)

K2, p1 rib st, yarn A: 26 sts = 4"/10cm

INSTRUCTIONS

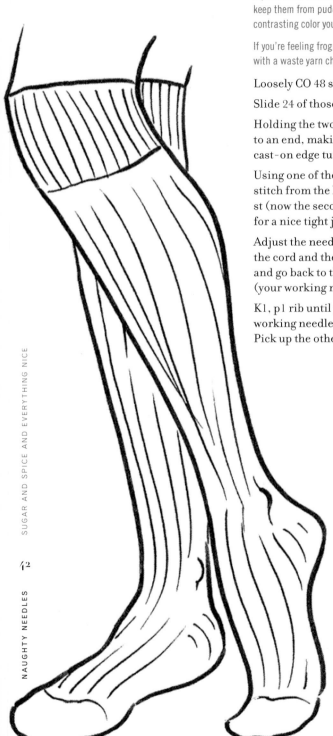

CUFF

Alpaca lacks the bounce-back memory of wool, so using wool near the top of the socks will keep them from puddling around your ankles. The cuff will conceal the wool part—or pick a contrasting color you like and wear the cuffs up—or knit the whole cuff in wool.

If you're feeling froggy, try the tubular cast-on ("Techniques," p. 136) for the cuff. You'll start with a waste yarn chain of 25 and use the even number variation before joining.

Loosely CO 48 sts in A.

Slide 24 of those sts onto your second needle.

Holding the two needles parallel, push all the sts on both needles down to an end, making sure the unconnected ends are at the top, with the cast-on edge turned toward the inside.

Using one of the opposite needle ends, work the join: Transfer the first stitch from the left needle onto the right. Then transfer the original first st (now the second st) on the right needle over and onto the left needle for a nice tight join. Essentially, the last two sts will have traded places.

Adjust the needle on the right so that its sts are resting in the middle of the cord and the pointy ends are hanging slack. Ignore them for now, and go back to the other needles. Pick up the slack end of the left needle (your working needle) and start your cuff!

K1, p1 rib until you run out of sts on that needle. Then adjust your working needle so the sts rest in the center of the cord; drop that needle. Pick up the other circulars and work the other half of the round.

Always work the first stitch on each set of needles *tightly* to prevent a loose ladder of stitches between.

Continue, alternating between needles, until you've knit 3"/7.5cm in K1, p1 rib.

Change to B. Knit 2"/5cm, finishing out your row.

LEG

This part will be zombie work, so pull out the *Buffy* Season 5 or *X-Files* Season 3 DVDs. (Bonus: Constantly switching your range of focus from your hands to the other side of the room will reduce eye strain, so it's good to have the TV or another low-attention visual distraction whenever you're knitting. But try to watch something you've seen before so you don't get too distracted.)

Change back to A. Switch to K2, p1 rib.

Continue in pattern until total length is 18"/45.5cm, then shift both needles so all stitches are in centers of cords and try on your sock! The live end should rest at

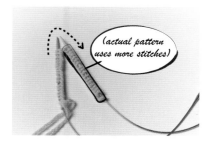

(actual pattern uses more stitches)

CO and divide stitches between two needles.

(use other ends of needles to help slip stitches)

Slide them all to one end, then slip the last stitch on each needle to the opposite needle, creating a firm join.

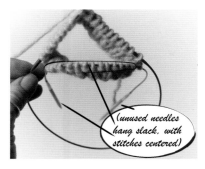

(unused needles hang slack, with stitches centered)

You'll work half the stitches at a time with one pair of circular needles, while the other pair hangs slack. When you finish up the row, slide the stitches to the center, pick up the slack pair, and keep knitting.

your ankles. These should be nice and long, probably mid-knee or higher, depending on your legs. Especially long or plump legs, or muscular calves, might warrant an extra inch or two to allow the cuff to fold over (mine did . . . let's just call them "muscular"). If you like this length, proceed to the heel flap! Otherwise, knit on until you're satisfied.

HEEL

WORKING THE HEEL

If you're a sock novice, find a nice quiet place to work the heel. Turn off the TV and close your door (or go sit on the roof or under a tree or in the laundry room or wherever it is no one will bother you). At this point, you have one long tube. Now you'll add a flap to one half of your tube. You'll knit the heel flap using your first needle, back and forth, like it's regular, flat knitting. You'll just drop that other needle and forget about it for a while.

Before you get started, transfer one stitch from the beginning of each needle (the K2 edge) to the other needle (so you'll slip one stitch at either end where the needles meet). Now your pattern on both needles will start with K1, p1 and end with P1, k1. This just keeps your pattern nice and tidy. Presto!

It's important to maintain a slipped-stitch edge for when you knit the gusset (that's where the heel flap meets up with the top of the sock to make a foot shape). You'll see a neat chain emerge on either side instead of a knotty-looking stockinette st edge.

HEEL FLAP

All rows: Starting with the yarn in front, you'll slip 1 st purlwise (inserting your right needle from the right, as if you're about to purl), move your yarn to the back, and continue as directed. On purled rows, you must also end each row with 1 knit st (the knit rows will naturally end in one already). (For tips, see Basic Top, p. 21.)

Row 1 (knit row): Sl 1, *k1, Sl 1 knitwise, repeat from *, ending row with k 1—24 sts.

Row 2 (purl row): Sl 1, p to last st from end, k last st.

Repeat both rows 10 times.

TURNING HEEL

So, you have a long tube with a squarish flap hanging off one half. The flap will run down the back of your heel. Now you'll work the curved part of the sock where the back of your heel meets the bottom of your foot.

Row 1: Sl 1, k13, k2tog, k1, turn.

Row 2: Sl 1, p5, p2tog, p1, turn.

Row 3: Sl 1, k6, k2tog, k1, turn

Row 4: Sl 1, p7, p2tog, p1, turn.

Row 5: Sl 1, k8, k2tog, k1, turn.

Row 6: Sl 1, p9, p2tog, p1, turn.

Row 7: Sl 1, k10, k2tog, k1, turn

Row 8: Sl 1, p11, p2tog, p1, turn.

Row 9: Sl 1, k12, k2tog, turn.

Row 10: Sl 1, p12, k2tog (to maintain edge), turn.

Row 11: Sl 1, k13.

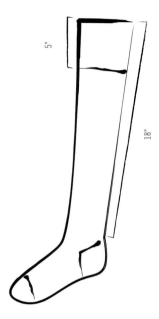

PICKING UP THE GUSSET

Now for the exciting part! If this is your first sock and you haven't already started the "Look—a sock!" chorus, this is where you'll find yourself holding it up in amazement every five to seven minutes and exclaiming, "Look! It's a sock! Look at it! It's exactly like a sock!" If you have company, they will find your enthusiasm tiresome long before you finish the gusset. But you won't. After all, it's freakin' magic! Look! A sock!

You've got a tube and a flap with a very shallow bowl at the end of it. When you pick up the gusset, you're going to bring that bowl around under your heel and connect the bottom of the sock with the back sides of the heel and taper down to the arch.

Using the same needle you used in that last row, pick up and knit into the 12 chain sts formed along the edge of the heel flap. (Skip the one immediately below.)

Now, stop right there. Slide all the sts on this needle to its opposite end/point, then transfer 7 of those sts on that end (opposite end from what you just worked) to your *other* needle (the one that's been hanging slack). Slide the transferred sts back to the middle of the needle so they don't go anywhere. It will look weird and wrong, with a big gap in space between its original row of sts and the one you've just transferred, but everything will come together in a minute.

Go back to the needle you were just working, the one with the flap, and slide your work so your working needle tip is back at the live end. Lift the bar that forms the intersection from front to back just like you were about to do a M1 increase, only don't knit it yet. (On the next round, you'll knit through the back loop of it to twist it and keep a gaping hole from forming there, just as you would with an M1 increase—but delayed.)

Place marker.

Right now, you're at the side of the sock. Up to this point, you've been working the sock in two halves: back and front. After this, you'll be working the sock from both sides instead. To get there, for the one and only time, you're going to knit using near ends of both pairs of circular needles.

Holding the flap needle in your right hand and the other in your left, knit in pattern into the first 12 sts. Now you're right at the top center of where the foot of the sock begins. You'll have a total of 32 sts on your needle, and you'll never mix needles again.

Slide the completed sts to the center of their needle, and drop that needle to work with the other one, just as you did when forming the leg. Knit the rest of the top of the sock (12 more sts in pattern). Place a marker. You now have a marker at either side of your foot. Lift up the intersection bar as you did with the other side, then pick up and knit the 12 sts up the remaining edge of the heel flap.

Once you've joined up the heel flap, you'll find those previously awkward-looking transferred sts waiting neatly for you. Knit them as well. You'll now have 32 sts on this needle, too. And now, instead of having the front of the sock on one needle and the back on the other, you've redistributed all your sts so you have the left half on one and the right half on the other.

Go on to the other needles. K7, k10 **tbl**, k2tog **tbl**, k1 **tbl**, SM work in pattern on 12 sts to end of needle. Switch needles to continue rib pattern on 12 sts, SM, K1 **tbl**, ssk **tbl**, k10 **tbl**, k7.

WORKING THE GUSSET

This is where you form that dart-like taper that follows your foot from heel to arch.

Rnd 1: K16, k2tog, k1, 24 sts in rib pattern (12 on each needle), k1, ssk, k16.

Rnd 2: (and every even rnd): K across, maintaining rib pattern.

Rnd 3: (and every odd round): Keep decreasing as above. Knit 1 less st than in previous rnd, k2tog, k1, 24 sts in rib pattern, k1, ssk, k1 less st than in previous rnd.

Continue until odd-numbered (dec) row gives you a total of 24 sts on each needle.

FOOT

Knit in pattern for about 2"/5cm, then try the sock on for size. Continue knitting until it goes to the big knuckle joint at the side of your big toe. Make sure you complete the row.

TOE

Knit all stitches, decreasing twice per needle (4x total) every other round.

Rnd 1: K9, k2tog, k2, ssk, k9. Repeat on 2nd needle.

Rnd 2 (and every even round): Knit.

Rnd 3 (and every odd round): K 1 less st than previous rnd, k2tog, k2, ssk, k 1 less than previous rnd. Repeat on 2nd needle. Continue until you have 10 sts on each needle, then k1 more row.

Exchange the last sts on both sides as you did when you first joined the rnd. Graft in kitchener stitch. Hurrah!

Go make the other one!

STRIPE IT RICH

Let self-striping yarn do all the work (as shown here). Kinderwhore uses a bigger gauge than typical socks, so you'll need to use two strands of thin sock yarn (match up yarn patterns first), or carry a strand of lace weight yarn along with thicker sock yarn. Option 1: 4 balls Sock It To Me Collection Harlequin (50g; 230 yd/210m; 75% superwash wool, 25% nylon) 79 polar ice. Work doubled. Option 2: 2 balls Lion Brand Magic Stripes (100g; 330 yd/300m; 75% wool, 25% nylon) 310-200 jelly bean worked together with 1 hank Knit Picks Alpaca Cloud (50g; 440yd/402m; 100% baby alpaca) 23495 smoke.

Lolita

Inspired by a failed sock experiment, these
dandy little garters sass up (and hold up) the
plainest (and limpest) of socks. Not just for
knee-highs, they can moonlight with stockings
or trousers (keeping your pants leg out of your
bicycle chain) or be worn as a fetching choker
or wristlet (wrapped twice). With minimal
yarn requirements and instant gratification,
this project is both the perfect stashbuster and
the perfect last-minute giftie. The girly set
below uses Fembot leftovers for thrifty bling.

Make matching sock garters with the leftovers
from your next gift project for a darling set.
Snap the garters together from end to end
and slip around a garment or gift box for
extra cuteness.

SIZING
One size (or custom)

YARN, ETC.
15 yd/14m Cascade *Fixation* (full ball = 50g; 100yd/91.5cm; 98.3% cotton, 1.7% elastic) (A)

20 yd/18m Karabella *Gossamer* (full ball = 50g; 222yd/203m; 30% kid mohair, 52% nylon, 18% polyester) (B)

2 slide-lock type bra fasteners (front-closure type)

NEEDLES & NOTIONS
US 3/3.25mm needles

Smallest pom-pom maker (I like Clover's Pom-pom Maker)

GAUGE
Gauge isn't critical here

INSTRUCTIONS

With an 8"/20cm tail, CO 5 st with A and knit all rows, slipping first st every row.

Continue until band is 9"/23cm long (or 3"/8cm less than your knee measurement, for custom fit). BO, leaving an 8"/20cm tail.

Feed edges through fastener and sew down through the purl bumps with the tails. Make sure you're keeping both of the fastener fronts facing properly before you sew it all down. Weave in ends.

Make 2 small pom-poms, leaving 6"/15cm long tails. Sew tails into garter 1 st apart, knot ends together on inside at a length that suits you, then weave in ends.

Folks who bike to the office will appreciate a simple no-nonsense wool version to keep their trousers out of their bicycle chains—skip the pom-poms and use 8 yd/7.5m of bouncy plied merino with plenty of stretch in the strand.

Zelda

This two-tone flapper-inspired garter slip has gorgeous drape and a luxurious touch, thanks to its silk and cashmere blend yarn. It's edged in seed stitch, with a slender panel of simple lace down the center. Its elegant, understated styling and sexy garter clips make it a lovely trousseau gift. But if the thought of all that work being sequestered in the honeymoon suite makes you pout, make it a bit longer and wear it as a dress (just be sure your panties match, as the lace will give you a hint of lookie-here action). Use an extra ball or two of yarn and add 6–10"/15–25cm to the bottom before starting the decrease.

SIZING
Women's S (M, L, XL)

Where no parentheses are used, instructions/quantities apply to all sizes

YARN, ETC.
3 (3, 4, 4) balls Karabella *Breeze* (50g; 202yd/185m; 60% silk, 40% cashmere), 32 apricot (A)

1 ball Karabella *Breeze* (50g; 202yd/185m; 60% silk, 40% cashmere), 28 ecru (B)

4 clear garter tabs

NEEDLES & NOTIONS
US 4/3.5mm needles, or for gauge

Sharp darning needle

Safety pins

GAUGE
ALWAYS CHECK YOUR GAUGE! Measure unwashed and unblocked, just relaxed and patted flat (NOT smoothed out)

Stockinette st: 22 sts = 4"/10cm

If you're looking for a substitute yarn, consider fiber content as well as gauge. You'll want a yarn with at least 50% of a non-stretching fiber, such as silk, cotton, rayon, linen, or bamboo. Treat a strict vegan to a silky 100% bamboo version.

Eliminating the second color doesn't increase the required number of main-color balls.

INSTRUCTIONS

The lace pattern is worked over 6 rows, with stockinette stitch on either side and various decreases and shaping happening around it. For simplicity, it is noted with a [lace] placeholder in the instructions; you'll track it independently, always working it in 6-row sets. But don't worry—most of the other pattern activity (shaping, armholes, etc.) corresponds to lace sets, which are referenced in the pattern, so you won't ever be fighting the lace. You'll either find directions in 6-row increments or 2-row increments that repeat over the duration of the lace.

LACE PATTERN

Please count your stitches during or after every lace panel so you won't have far to unknit if you mess up. Because the yarn overs and passed stitches can be difficult to decipher and therefore difficult to pick back up, it's best to unknit, one stitch at a time, rather than frogging.

Row 1 (RS): P1, k1, *yo, k2, sl 1, k2tog, psso, k2, yo, k1, repeat from *, p1.

Row 2 (WS): K1, p17, k1.

Row 3: P1, k2, yo, k1, sl 1, k2tog, psso, k1, yo, k3, yo, k1, sl 1, k2tog, psso, k1, yo, k2, p1.

Row 4: Repeat Row 2.

Row 5: P1, k3, yo, sl 1, k2tog, psso, yo, k5, yo, sl 1, k2tog, psso, yo, k3, P1.

Row 6: Repeat Row 2.

FRONT

CO 38 (42, 48, 54) sts, PM, CO 19 sts, PM, CO 38 (42, 48, 54) sts—95 (103, 115, 127) sts.

HEMLINE—6 ROWS

Row 1 (RS): *K1, p1, repeat from * to marker, [lace], *p1, k1, repeat from * to end.

Row 2 (WS): * K1, p1, repeat from * to marker, [lace], * p1, k1, repeat to end.

Repeat 2 more times, finishing out the 6-row lace set flanked by seed stitch.

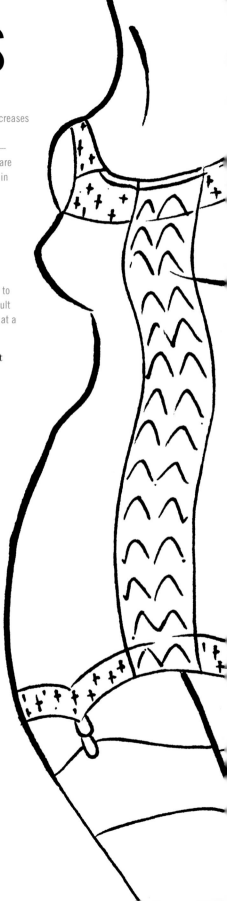

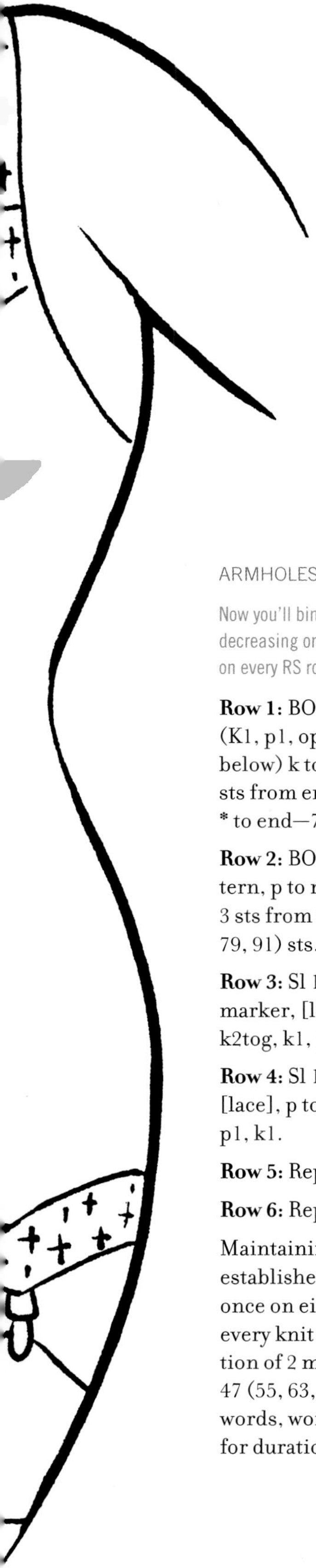

SKIRT DECREASE—96 (96, 102, 102) ROWS

Now you'll decrease once on either side, 3 sts in. Use ssk on the first side and k2tog on the other side.

Continue all rows in stockinette st and lace as established until you've finished 3 repeats of the lace pattern (18 rows).

Repeat entire 18-row set 2 more times—89 (97, 109, 121) sts.

Now, decrease as above on either end of the first row of each lace set (first of 6 rows).

Repeat dec row every 6th row 2 (2, 3, 3) times more—83 (91, 101, 113) sts.

TORSO—30 (30, 36, 36) ROWS

Work even (stockinette with 6-row lace panel) for 4 (4, 5, 5) more lace sets—24 (24, 30, 30) rows.

Start a final lace set as normal. On the last row (WS), work as usual until 10 sts from edge, *p 1, k1, repeat from * to end.

ARMHOLES—18 ROWS

Now you'll bind off the underarms and begin decreasing once on either side, 3 stitches in, on every RS row a total of 8 times.

Row 1: BO 10 sts in seed st pattern (K1, p1, opposite of previous sts below) k to marker, [lace], k to 10 sts from end, *p1, k1, repeat from * to end—73 (81, 91, 103) sts.

Row 2: BO 10 sts in seed st pattern, p to marker, [lace], p to 3 sts from end, k1, p1, k1—63 (71, 79, 91) sts.

Row 3: Sl 1, p1, k1, ssk, k to marker, [lace], k to 5 sts from end, k2tog, k1, p1, k1.

Row 4: Sl 1, p1, k1, p to marker, [lace], p to last 3 sts from end, k1, p1, k1.

Row 5: Repeat Row 3.

Row 6: Repeat Row 4.

Maintaining 3 sts in pattern as established, continue to decrease once on either side 3 sts in on every knit (RS) row for the duration of 2 more lace sets (12 rows)—47 (55, 63, 75) sts. (In other words, work rows 3 and 4 above for duration of 2 lace sets.)

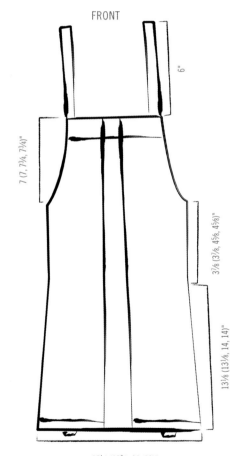

FRONT

7 (7, 7¾, 7¾)"

6"

3⅞ (3⅞, 4⅝, 4⅝)"

13⅛ (13⅛, 14, 14)"

17¼ (18¾, 21, 23)"

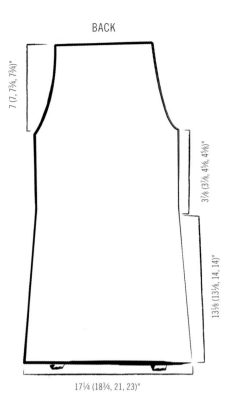

BACK

7 (7, 7¾, 7¾)"

3⅞ (3⅞, 4⅝, 4⅝)"

13⅛ (13⅛, 14, 14)"

17¼ (18¾, 21, 23)"

Row 1: Sl 1, p1, k to marker, [lace], k to 2 st from end, p1, k1.

Row 2: Sl 1, p1, k1, p to marker, [lace], p to last 3 st from end, k1, p1, k1.

Repeat both rows twice to finish out each lace set. The continue repeating until you've completed 3 (3, 4, 4) lace sets total—18 (18, 24, 24) rows.

Change to B, and repeat Rows 1 and 2 with lace pattern to complete 2 more lace sets (12 rows).

NECKLINE—6 ROWS

Switch back to A, sl 1, *p1, k1, repeat from * across row.

Sl 1, p1, k1, p1, k1, BO 37 (45, 53, 65) sts, k1, p1, k1, p1, k1.

STRAPS

All strap rows: Sl 1, p1, k1, p1, k1. Work 6"/15cm and transfer live stitches to safety pin. Break yarn, leaving 1 yd/1m tail.

BACK

The front and back must have the same number of rows up to the armholes to avoid any surprises in the seaming. It's a good idea to count the total number of rows up to the armhole bindoff. That way, if you've goofed at all, you can make the necessary adjustments when you knit the back.

CO 95 (103, 115, 127) sts.

Work as for front, replacing lace panel with plain stockinette/seed st. When you reach the color change, continue with A instead, work 2 rows in seed st and BO in pattern.

FINISHING

GARTERS

Using pins or locking stitch markers, mark hemline 5 (5½, 6, 6½)"/12.5 (14, 15, 16.5)cm. out from edge of lace panel on either side. From center back, mark 6½ (7, 7½, 8)"/16.5 (18, 19, 20.5)cm out on either side.

Pick up and knit 4 sts from inside (WS) hemline, 4 rows up, centered over each marked spot. K4 rows in stockinette st and BO, leaving 8"/20cm tail. Slip garter tab over nub, and seam down. Repeat with 3 other garter markers.

SIDES AND STRAPS

Seam sides.

Pin live strap sts on safety pins to same position in back. Try on slip and adjust straps as necessary, unraveling or knitting more for best fit. Seam to back.

Dirty Secrets

These gorgeous secret-compartment boudoir pillows let you simply and economically showcase that fabulous handspun yarn you've been hoarding. To help you rationalize buying the fancy stuff, they're backed with yarn from your stash or inexpensive wool or novelty yarn and lined with frugal cotton. Both pillows boast hidden compartments so your favorite bedroom toys (or whatever else you like) can hide in plain sight. The larger oblong pillow is not only stylishly proportioned, but roomy enough to conceal your Magic Wand. The square toss pillow holds a Rabbit, Hello Kitty vibe, or similar battery-powered toy. If you don't fancy the power tools, either pillow can conceal lube, condoms, breath mints, earplugs, a sleep mask, your diary, mad money—whatever you wish. Bring one of these babies, fully loaded, to a bachelorette or birthday party and you'll be the Best! Friend! Ever!

Yarn requirements are included for three general weights, and they're noted parenthetically, as sizes would be for a garment. If you run out of yarn early, simply adjust your pillow back and liner by reducing the overall length of each.

YARN, ETC.
Handspun quantities and needles sizes are given for 3 weights.

150 (130, 110) yd/137 (119, 110)m Hello Yarn or Maisy Day *Handspun,* heavy worsted (bulky, superbulky) (varying weights and fiber contents) (A)

1 hank Blue Sky Alpacas *Dyed Cotton* (100g; 150yd/137m; 100% organically grown cotton) or 1 ball Lily *Sugar and Cream* (70g; 120yd/109m; 100% cotton), color of your choice (B)

1 ball Patons *Classic Merino Wool* (100g; 223yd/205m; 100% merino wool), color of your choice (C)

Cluster Stuff stuffing

Hi-loft poly batting
(Batting and stuffing available at craft and fabric stores; one package of each will more than accommodate several projects)

1"/2.5cm button (optional)

OPTIONAL, FOR FELTED PILLOWS
Embroidery floss to match backing fabric

NEEDLES & NOTIONS
US 10/6mm, 11/8mm, or 13/9mm needles for heavy worsted, bulky, or superbulky, respectively, or for gauge

US 8/5mm 16"/40.5cm circular needles, or for gauge

Large, sharp embroidery needle

OPTIONAL (FOR CROCHETED SEAM)
I/9, L/11, or N/13 crochet hook for heavy worsted, bulky, or superbulky, respectively

GAUGE
ALWAYS CHECK YOUR GAUGE! Measure unwashed and unblocked, just relaxed and patted flat (NOT smoothed out)

[1] Stockinette st, A heavy worsted (bulky, superbulky) on larger needles:

15 (13, 10) = 4"/10cm

[2] Stockinette st, C on smaller needles: 16 sts = 4"/10cm

[3] Stockinette st, B on smaller needles: about 20 sts = 4"/10cm (gauge is not too critical)

INSTRUCTIONS

If you plan to machine felt and you're using a button loop, either make the loop out of cotton or wrap a bit of similar-colored cotton yarn around it. The cotton won't felt, and will keep your loop from becoming a weird blobby mole on the back of your pillow.

Since the Rabbit and similar vibes are made of sticky silicone, you'll want to use a vinyl makeup bag inside your pillow to keep them from looking like lint removers.

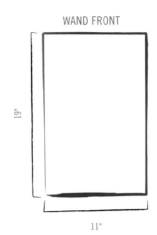

WAND FRONT

19"

11"

FRONT

For Magic Wand Pillow:

With A and larger needles, CO 41 (36, 25) sts.

Knit 19"/48.5cm in stockinette st and BO.

For Rabbit Pillow:

With A and larger needles, CO 45 (39, 30) sts.

Knit 12"/30.5cm in stockinette st and BO.

BACK (2 PIECES)

For Magic Wand Pillow:

With B and smaller needles, CO 44 sts.

Knit 18"/45.5cm in stockinette st, ending with RS row.

Work 3 rows in garter st and BO.

With B and smaller needles, CO 44 sts.

Knit 3"/8 cm in stockinette st, ending with RS row.

Work 3 rows in garter st and BO.

For Rabbit Pillow:

With B and smaller needles, CO 48 sts.

Knit 10½"/26.5cm in stockinette st, ending with RS row.

Work 3 rows in garter st and BO.

With B and smaller needles, CO 48 sts.

Knit 3"/7.5cm in stockinette st, ending with RS row.

Work 3 rows in garter st and BO.

LINER

For Magic Wand Pillow:

With C and smaller needles, CO 70 sts.

Knit 17"/43cm in stockinette st and BO.

Fold over lengthwise. Seam side and bottom.

WAND LINER

17"

7"

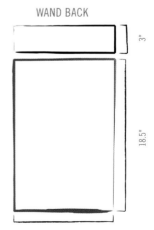

WAND BACK

3"

18.5"

11"

RABBIT LINER

10"

8"

RABBIT FRONT

12" square

RABBIT BACK

3"

11"

12"

For Rabbit Pillow:

With C and smaller needles, CO 80 sts.

Knit 10"/25.5cm in stockinette st and BO.

Fold over lengthwise. Seam side and bottom.

FINISHING

Weave in all ends.

Block pillow top and backs.

Using leftover cotton, baste front and backs together so that stockinette edges of backs align with pillow top sides, and garter sides overlap (see open pillow picture to better understand). Seam all 4 sides with your favorite seam. Crocheting around the edges with the handspun has a nice look, but any good seam will work. Remove the cotton basting.

BUTTON LOOP (OPTIONAL)

If you like, pick up and knit 2 sts, ½"/13mm from center of smaller back flap. Knit a 1½–2"/3.8–5cm I-cord. BO and seam 1"/2.5cm away from picked-up side, ½"/13mm from center in the other direction. This will be your button loop. (Alternately, use a crocheted chain.)

STUFFING AND LINING

If you're felting the cover, felt, block, and dry completely before proceeding.

Cut 2 pieces of batting, twice the width of your liner + 2"/5cm and the length of your liner + 1"/2.5cm.

Fold both layers around the tube and baste shut with a couple of sts at the side and bottom. Carefully insert the batted liner into the pillow cover, then use the Cluster Stuff to fill in all the voids and make it nice and fluffy. Do not overstuff or your toys won't fit, but don't understuff, or they won't be well-concealed. Place future contents in the pouch while you stuff the pillow.

With pillow back yarn and a sharp needle, sew one side of liner (the side touching the pillow back) down to the 2nd row of purl bumps on the inside of the pillow back garter edge. Also using the pillow back yarn, sew the opposite end of the tube down to the second row of purls on the wrong side of the stockinette/seam end of the small pillow back piece.

Condom Critter

She's darling and whimsical—and look, she's safeguarding your condoms in her little pouch! What a dear. But that's not all. This cuddly creature is also a clever cozy. Her goofy legs are drawstrings for a hidden compartment, sized to stash a bottle of lube, small vibe, or your iPod. A friend, indeed! Like Dirty Secrets, she's designed to showcase gorgeous one-of-a-kind handspun. The meager yarn requirements make this perfect for those little hanks of handspun yarn you often see but don't buy because they seem too small to actually yield anything. She's knit in reverse stockinette stitch so you want very irregular yarn—the more slubs and bubbles, the better!

YARN, ETC.

Handspun quantities are given for 2 weights.

50 (100) yd/45 (91)m Hello Yarn or Maisy Day *Handspun*, superbulky (bulky) thick-and-thin yarn (weight and content will vary) (A)

1 hank Blue Sky Alpacas *Dyed Cotton* (100g; 150yd/137m; 100% organically grown cotton) or 1 ball Lily *Sugar and Cream* (70g; 120yd/109m; 100% cotton), color of your choice (B)

Cluster Stuff stuffing

Hi-loft poly batting
(Batting and stuffing available at fabric and craft stores—one package of each will more than accommodate several projects)

Felt scraps

Google eyes or plain buttons

Sewing thread or craft glue

You can get away with slightly less yarn by just skipping the pocket or making her somewhat smaller. CO 20 sts instead of 26 and k 5"/13cm instead of 6"/15cm stockinette, and knit the cotton tube just 5½"/14cm deep.

NEEDLES & NOTIONS
US 15/10mm needle, or to obtain fabric you like

US 5/3.75mm double pointed needles

Point protectors

Sharp darning needle

Sewing needle (unless using craft glue)

GAUGE
ALWAYS CHECK YOUR GAUGE! Measure unwashed and unblocked, just relaxed and patted flat (NOT smoothed out)

Stockinette st, A superbulky (or bulky, doubled) on larger needles: 8–11 st = 4"/10cm (gauge is not too critical)

INSTRUCTIONS

If you're using the bulky weight, knit with 2 strands held together.

With larger needle and B used as waste yarn, CO 26 sts.

Wind 2 yd/2.2m yarn A into a butterfly or onto a bobbin, then continue knitting, dropping waste yarn.

Knit 6"/15cm in stockinette, ending in k row.

*P2, p2tog repeat from *, ending with p2—20 sts.

Work 2 rows in stockinette st.

*K1, k2tog, yo, k1 repeat from * to end.

P1 row. Break yarn.

Switch to smaller needles (use double-pointed needles as straight needles, with point protectors on ends) and B (dropping A).

*K tbl across row.

Work 7"/18cm in k2, p2 rib.

Break yarn, leaving 4"/10cm tail.

Seam bottom and side of ribbed tube, leaving long tail.

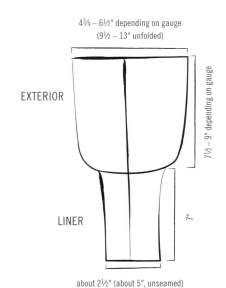

EXTERIOR

LINER

4¾ – 6½" depending on gauge
(9½ – 13" unfolded)

7½ – 9" depending on gauge

7"

about 2½" (about 5", unseamed)

POUCH

With A and large needles, *loosely* CO 14 sts.

Sl 1, k to end.

Sl 1, p2tog, p8, p2tog, k1.

Sl 1, k to end.

Sl 1, p2tog, p6, p2tog, k1.

Work 5 rows stockinette st, always slipping first stitch and knitting last.

Sl 1, p2tog, p4, p2tog, k1.

BO knitwise.

FINISHING

Using reverse stockinette st as right side, position pocket (also with reverse stockinette as right side) near or at center and whip-stitch in place with A.

Remove waste yarn from CO end by snipping and unraveling, and transfer the 26 live sts to larger needle as you unravel.

With stockinette st facing out and face and pouch facing in, slip the first 6 sts to double-pointed needle (without point protectors or rubber bands), slip next 13 sts to second double-pointed needle, then slip remaining 7 sts to opposite end of first dpn. One dpn will hold 13 consecutive sts, the other will hold 13 consecutive sts with a gap in the middle

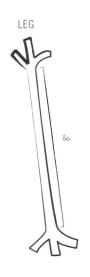

LEG

8"

where the back seam will occur. Once you have sts set up, put the point protectors or rubber bands back on one side to keep the stitches from slipping off.

Unwind bobbin of A and thread yarn needle. Weave it through row directly under live sts until you've reached the working end of the needles. Then, starting on one end, close open edges with kitchener st (see "Techniques," p. 131). Do not break tail.

The top will be seamed with corners, the middle back will have an open slit, and the bottom will terminate in a sock-like closed ribbed tube.

Turn RS (reverse stockinette st) out. Tug the points out on the top of the head so they stand up.

Invert tube so it's inside the body, puppet-fashion.

Double the batting and slip it inside the critter, wrapping it around the ribbed section so it forms a padded tube. Baste the batting tube shut with the sharp needle and some leftover B.

Fill in the rest of the body medium-loosely with batting, making sure it is completely enclosed without overstuffing. You should be able to stick your hand firmly up the ribbed tube.

Seam up the back with the remaining A tail, and weave in ends.

LEGS

Using double-pointed needles and B, CO 3 sts.

Knit 4—6 rows of I-cord. Break yarn and transfer to safety pin. Repeat.

CO 3 sts. Knit 5 rows I-cord, then transfer one of the little cords to either end of the live cord.

Treating all 3 pieces as one, k2, k2tog, k1, k2tog, k2—7 sts. The k2tog decreases combine the end sts at the joints where the individual cords meet.

Work 1 row I-cord, then (k2tog) three times, k1—4 sts.

Continue 4-stitch I-cord until it has reached 8"/20.5cm. Break yarn, leaving 3 yd/3.3m tail.

Continue knitting using tail. Now you'll increase by picking up and knitting into the bars between the stitches to make a total of 9 stitches over 2 rows.

K1, M1, k1, M1, k1, M1, k1.

K2, M1, k3, M1, k2.

Transfer the 6 sts on the right to safety pin.

Using the 3 remaining stitches only, continue in I-cord for 5 rows and BO.

With yarn needle, feed yarn tail through center of I-cord toe and up to first live st. Continue to knit, with the tail as the working yarn.

Repeat process, 3 sts at a time, for remaining 2 toes.

FINISHING

Weave in yarn ends. Carefully work feet/leg cord through eyelet holes formed from yarn over in bottom of owl's body, starting and ending at front center holes. Legs form drawstring closure.

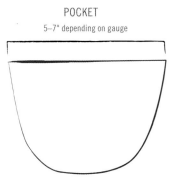

POCKET
5—7" depending on gauge

Ice Vixen vs. Cave Girl

One of the great triumphs of old B movies is their innovative (cynics might say gratuitous) use of bikinis. These days, B movies resort to ordinary, uninspired nudity, but the bikinis of yore were much more fun. Some of the best bikinis were the furry pelt bikinis worn by cave girls, Amazons, and wild women, usually along with long, disheveled hair and long, suntanned legs. Since Raquel Welch's One Million Years BC bikini requires more architecture than what comes standard on the average human woman, I turned to Bunny Yeager, the classic pinup photographer, for design inspiration. She designed many of the suits that her famous bikini girls wore. Her daring, sexy creations were quite racy for an era that championed bullet-bra and girdle proportions in swimwear—but still left plenty of room for imagination.

Both versions are knit with the same pattern, but the qualities of yarn and stitch give the two versions slightly different proportions. The pieces may look kind of huge until you actually try them on (modern swimwear and underwear are terribly skimpy, so they'll distort your expectations).

SIZING
WOMEN'S S (M, L, XL)
Where no parentheses are used, instructions/quantities apply to all sizes

YARN, ETC.
For Ice Vixen (white)
4 (5, 6, 6) balls Berroco *Softy* (50g; 104yds/96m; 52% DuPont Tactel nylon, 48% nylon), 2901 snow bunny (A)

1 ball Cascade *Fixation* (50g; 100yd/91.5m; 98.3% cotton, 1.7% elastic), 8176 ecru (B)

For Cave Girl (brown)
2 (3, 3, 4) balls Patons *Divine* (100g; 142yd/129m; 79.5% acrylic, 18% mohair, 2.5% polyester), 06013 deep earth (A)

1 card Tejas Lace Company *Suede Lace* (⅛" x 8yd/7.3m; 100% suede leather), 02 dark brown

NEEDLES & NOTIONS
US 35/19mm needle (just 1)

US 10.5/6.5mm needles, or for gauge

FOR ICE VIXEN ONLY
US 2–4/2.75–3.5mm double-pointed needles (gauge is not critical for straps)

GAUGE
ALWAYS CHECK YOUR GAUGE!
Measure unwashed and unblocked, just relaxed and patted flat (NOT smoothed out)

Stockinette st, A on middle needles: 12½ sts = 4"/10cm

65

INSTRUCTIONS

If you don't feel like knitting the I-cord, you can substitute ivory or beige suede or deerskin lace. If you do, be sure to use the Cave Girl measurements, as the leather straps need additional length to compensate for the lack of stretch.

If you're sensitive to mohair but like the Cave Girl look, try Patons *Carmen* (50g; 64yd/58m; 36% polyester, 64% nylon) in 07013 chocolate. It's not quite as primitive, but still has a nice, softly variegated fur effect, but in a slippery, soft synthetic. You'll need 4 (6, 6, 8) balls, since they're shorter.

If you really want to go whole hog with this fur pelt theme, randomly double your strand or add other mohair or eyelash/fun fur strands in randomly as you knit. You could even weave in strips of real fur (most craft stores sell bunny pelts). Then, dirty up your legs and face, rat your hair and throw a bone in it, speak in monosyllables, and pound on stuff—you're set!

Top

STRAPS

For Ice Vixen:

Using B and double-pointed needles, CO 3 sts and make a 30"/76cm I-cord. BO, leaving 16"/40cm tail. Repeat for second strap.

CO 4 sts and make a 50"/127cm I-cord. BO and weave in yarn ends.

For Cave Girl:

Cut two 40"/101.5cm strips and two 50"/127cm strips from leather lacing. You'll use 1 strip for each top strap and both 50"/127cm strips together for chest strap.

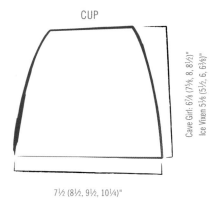

CUP

Cave Girl: 6⅞ (7⅝, 8, 8½)"
Ice Vixen 5⅛ (5½, 6, 6⅜)"

7½ (8½, 9½, 10¼)"

CUPS (MAKE 2)

For all rows, always slip the first stitch purlwise and knit the last stitch. The Ice Vixen will be knit in garter stitch, while the Cave Girl is knit in stockinette stitch, giving it longer proportions.

Using **(2 strands for Ice Vixen or 1 strand for Cave Girl)** A and US 35 needle, CO 24 (27, 30, 33) sts.

Switch to US 10.5 needles and knit 14 (16, 18, 20) rows.

Next row: Slip 1, k1 ssk, k to 4 st from edge, k2tog, k2.

Continue to dec as above (ssk/k2tog with the 3rd and 4th st in from either side) every other row until you hold 14 (17, 20, 23) sts.

BO with US 35 needle. Weave in yarn ends.

Repeat for second cup.

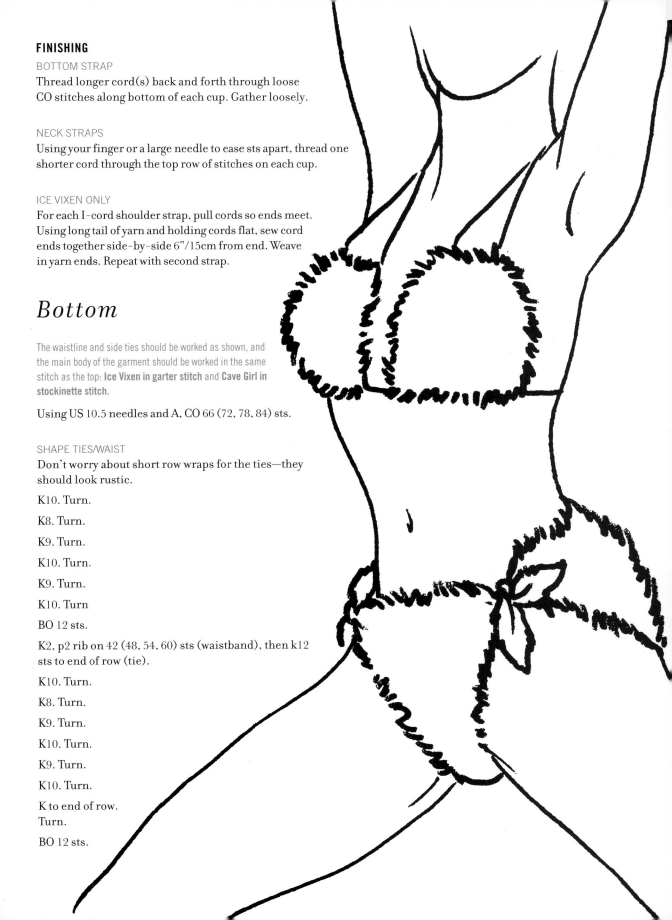

FINISHING

BOTTOM STRAP

Thread longer cord(s) back and forth through loose
CO stitches along bottom of each cup. Gather loosely.

NECK STRAPS

Using your finger or a large needle to ease sts apart, thread one
shorter cord through the top row of stitches on each cup.

ICE VIXEN ONLY

For each I-cord shoulder strap, pull cords so ends meet.
Using long tail of yarn and holding cords flat, sew cord
ends together side-by-side 6"/15cm from end. Weave
in yarn ends. Repeat with second strap.

Bottom

The waistline and side ties should be worked as shown, and
the main body of the garment should be worked in the same
stitch as the top: **Ice Vixen in garter stitch** and **Cave Girl in
stockinette stitch.**

Using US 10.5 needles and A, CO 66 (72, 78, 84) sts.

SHAPE TIES/WAIST

Don't worry about short row wraps for the ties—they
should look rustic.

K10. Turn.

K8. Turn.

K9. Turn.

K10. Turn.

K9. Turn.

K10. Turn

BO 12 sts.

K2, p2 rib on 42 (48, 54, 60) sts (waistband), then k12
sts to end of row (tie).

K10. Turn.

K8. Turn.

K9. Turn.

K10. Turn.

K9. Turn.

K10. Turn.

K to end of row.
Turn.

BO 12 sts.

Work to end of row, maintaining rib pattern.

Work 4 rows in k2, p2 rib.

BOTTOMS

13⅜ (15⅜, 17¼, 19¼)"

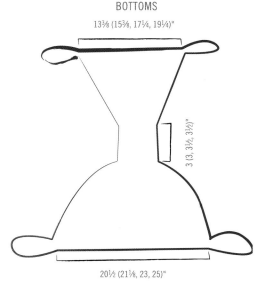

3 (3, 3½, 3½)"

20½ (21⅛, 23, 25)"

FRONT

Remainder of garment until k2, p2 rib at back waistband will be in style-specific stitch (**garter stitch for Ice Vixen** and **stockinette stitch for Cave girl**), with the first stitch of each row slipped and last stitch of each row knit. Decreases and increases will occur after the first 2 stitches at the beginning of the row and before the last 2 stitches at the end.

Sl 1, k1, ssk, knit to within 4 sts of end, k2tog, k2.

Repeat as above every other row until you have 10 (10, 12, 12) sts.

CROTCH

K (3, 3½, 3½)"/7.5 (7.5, 9, 9)cm, ending with WS row.

BACK

Use any increase you wish.

Sl 1, k1, inc 1st, work to within 2 stitches of end, inc 1st, K2.

Continue as above, every other row, until you have 40 (44, 48, 52) sts.

Thereafter, inc as above every 3rd row until 60 (66, 72, 78) sts. (**Cave Girl** will be placing some increases on purled rows.)

Thereafter, inc every 3rd row for **Cave Girl** and 6th row for **Ice Vixen** until 64 (70, 78, 84) sts.

SHAPE TIES/WAIST

4 rows k2, p2 rib.

CO 12 sts.

K10. Turn.

K8. Turn.

K9. Turn.

K10. Turn.

K9. Turn.

K10. Turn.

K to end of row, maintaining rib pattern along waist.

CO 12 sts. Turn.

K9. Turn.

K8. Turn.

K10. Turn.

K9. Turn.

K10. Turn.

K12. Turn.

BO, maintaining rib pattern along waist. Weave in ends.

Dirty Needles

WHEN I FINALLY found my perfect, sexually compatible partner, it was like an epiphany. The sex was so good, I couldn't stop talking about it—you would have thought I'd invented it myself. It's all I could think about, all day long. I developed what seemed like very important new theories about romantic bliss and filthy sex, and droned on and on about them to anyone who would listen.

I even ignored my Magic Wand.

New sex is always steamy. You're full of anticipation, all hotted up, and usually showing off. For new sex, you'll shave your legs. You'll take a shower and wear fancy underwear and change the sheets. You'll try new things without reservation. You'll do it upside down and backwards and on top of the refrigerator. You can barely watch a sitcom without pawing at each other, and *forget* seeing any movies all the way through. When you have new sex, you give it your all. And if you're very, very lucky, you keep giving it your all, and you keep getting surprised.

But even once you've found your perfect panty-melting partner who makes you feel like the champion Sexpot Queen of the Universe, there will be times when you're both busy or sloppy or tired or distracted. You'll neglect your diet. You'll neglect the sheets. You'll want to finish balancing your checkbook or reading the new *ReadyMade* or watching the end of *Lost*. And when those times threaten of take over, there's no better remedy than busting out the sexy threads. Parade around in your naughty clothes and you'll surely get a reward. After all, everyone loves a parade!

Whipping up your own little bedroom outfits is especially fun, not just because you get to answer "crotchless panties" when your prissy coworker asks what you're making, but because in hand-knitting them, you get to enjoy the luxury of anticipation.

These dirty little gems are fucktastic, but they all have a vintage flair and humor that makes them a bit more fun than your typical off-the-shelf dirties. And while you're working on your bedroom wardrobe, don't forget the more demure but equally fetching selections in the previous chapters, or the somewhat kinkier little treats in the chapters that follow.

. . . Parade around in your naughty clothes and you'll surely get a reward.

Criss-Cross Gloves and Garters

These little lace-up beauties have a very nostalgic naughtiness. The silky stockinette fabric is sleek; the seed stitch border, neatly offset with a crisp purl outline, is simple and elegant. Knit flat, neither garment is seamed; instead they lace up with satin ribbon through simple k2tog/YO eyelets.

　　Thanks to the lace-up sizes, the garter belt can be worn high or low on the hips, with the top resting just above the belly button or below the hip bones. It's scaled to leave a nice gap of skin showing between the two panels, and the front panel is slightly smaller than the back to bring the ties forward a bit. Skip the garter tabs (or leave them) for a saucy hip sash over a little black dress.

SIZING
Gloves: Women's one size

Garters: S (M, L, XL)
Where no parentheses are used, instructions/quantities apply to all sizes

YARN, ETC.
4 hanks Blue Sky Alpacas *Alpaca Silk* (50g; 146yd/133m; 50% alpaca, 50% silk), i50 night (each pattern uses 2 hanks)

4 yd/3.7m ⅜"/9mm satin ribbon, dusty rose (gloves)

4 yd/3.7m ⅝"/16mm satin ribbon, dusty rose (garter)

4 black garter clips (garter)

NEEDLES & NOTIONS
US 2/2.75mm needles, or for gauge

Stitch markers

GAUGE
Measure unwashed and unblocked, just relaxed and patted flat (NOT smoothed out)

Stockinette st: 25 sts = 4"/10cm

INSTRUCTIONS

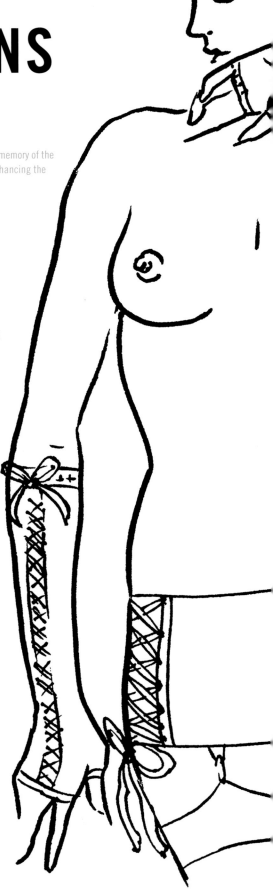

Gloves

These may look quite small as you're knitting them. Due to the low memory of the fibers, the seed st pattern will spread a fair amount in blocking, enhancing the stitching detail and enlarging the pieces.

CUFF

CO 37 sts.

Sl 1, *k1, p1, repeat from * to last 2 sts, k2.

Repeat 6 times for a total of 7 rows seed st with a smooth edge on either side.

Row 8 (WS): Sl 1, k1, p1, k1, p1, k1, k25, k1, p1, k1, p1, k2. This will show as a purl border between seed st and stockinette st on the right side.

WRIST

This will form a field of stockinette stitch flanked by a single column of purls and a seed stitch border, with eyelets every 4 rows and a smooth finished edge.

Row 1 (RS): Sl 1, k1, p1, k1, p2, k25, p2, k1, p1, k2.

Row 2 (WS) and all even rows: Sl 1, k1, p1, k1, p1, k1, p25, k1, p1, k1, p1, k2.

Row 3: Sl 1, k2tog, yo, k1, p2, k25, p2, k1, yo, k2tog, k1.

GLOVE

10½"

block to 6–6¼"

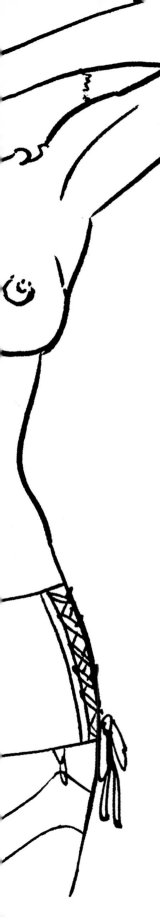

Row 4: Repeat Row 2.

Row 5: Repeat Row 1.

Row 6: Repeat Row 2.

Continue 6-row repeat for 8"/20.5cm, then as necessary to finish out set.

THUMB

Now you'll make a slightly offset thumb gusset, maintaining the edge/eyelet pattern. Then you'll trim the thumb, bind it off, and cast on 3 stitches to get you back to the same number you were knitting on the wrist. The thumb, the portion between the markers you place, is bolded for clarification.

Row 1 (RS): Sl 1, k1, p1, k1, p2, k14, PM, **[k3]**, PM, k8, p2, k1, p1, k2.

Row 2 (WS): Sl 1, k1, p1, k1, p1, k1, p8, **[p3]**, p14, k1, p1, k1, p1, k2.

Row 3: Sl 1, k2tog, yo, k1, p2, k14, **[M1, k3, M1]**, k8, p2, k1, yo, k2tog, k1.

Row 4: Sl 1, k1, p1, k1, p1, k1, p8, **[p5]**, p14, k1, p1, k1, p1, k2.

Row 5: Sl 1, k1, p1, k1, p2, k14, **[M1, k5, M1]**, k8, p2, k1, p1, k2.

Row 6: Sl 1, k1, p1, k1, p1, k1, p8, **[p7]**, p14, k1, p1, k1, p1, k2.

Row 7: Sl 1, k1, p1, k1, p2, k14, **[M1, k7, M1]**, k8, p2, k1, p1, k2.

Row 8: Sl 1, k1, p1, k1, p1, k1, p8, **[p9]**, p14, k1, p1, k1, p1, k2.

Row 9: Sl 1, k2tog, yo, k1, p2, k14, **[M1, k9, M1]**, k8, p2, k1, yo, k2tog, k1.

Row 10: Sl 1, k1, p1, k1, p1, k1, p8, **[p11]**, p14, k1, p1, k1, p1, p2.

Row 11: Sl 1, k1, p1, k1, p2, k14, **[M1, k11, m1]**, k8, p2, k1, p1, k2.

Row 12: Sl 1, k1, p1, k1, p1, k1, p8, **[p13]**, p14, k1, p1, k1, p1, k2.

Row 13: Sl 1, k1, p1, k1, p2, k14, **[M1, k13, M1]**, SM, k8, p2, k1, p1, k2.

Row 14: Sl 1, k1, p1, k1, p1, k1, p8, **[p15]**, p14, k1, p1, k1, p1, k2.

Row 15: Sl 1, k2tog, yo, k1, p2, k14, **[M1, *k1, p1, repeat from * 6 more times, k1, M1]**, k8, p2, k1, yo, k2tog, k1.

Row 16: Sl 1, k1, p1, k1, p1, k1, p8, **[* p1, k1, repeat from * 7 more times, p1]**, p14, k1, p1, k1, p1, k2.

Row 17: Sl 1, k1, p1, k1, p2, k14, **[M1, *p1 k1, repeat from * 7 more times, p1, M1]**, k8, p2, k1, p1, k2.

Row 18: Sl 1, k1, p1, k1, p1, k1, p8, (drop marker), **[BO 17 sts in seed]**, (drop marker), p13, k1, p1, k1, p1, k2.

Row 19: Sl 1, k1, p1, k1, p2, k14, **[CO 3 sts]**, k8, p2, k1, p1, k2.

Row 20: Sl 1, k1, p1, k1, p1, k1, 25, k1, p1, k1, p1, k2.

Proceed to *Hand*.

LEFT GLOVE

For the mate, you'll do the same, reversing the number of stitches before and after the thumb:

Row 1 (RS): Sl 1, k1, p1, k1, p2, k8, PM, **[k3]**, PM, k14, p2, k1, p1, k2.

Row 2 (WS): Sl 1, k1, p1, k1, p1, k1, p14, **[p3]**, p8, k1, p1, k1, p1, k2.

Row 3: Sl 1, k2tog, yo, k1, p2, k8, **[M1, k3, M1]**, k14, p2, k1, yo, k2tog, k1.

Row 4: Sl 1, k1, p1, k1, p1, k1, p14, **[p5]**, p8, k1, p1, k1, p1, k2.

Row 5: Sl 1, k1, p1, k1, p2, k8, **[M1, k5, M1]**, k14, p2, k1, p1, k2.

Row 6: Sl 1, k1, p1, k1, p1, k1, p14, **[p7]**, p8, k1, p1, k1, p1, k2.

Row 7: Sl 1, k1, p1, k1, p2, k8, **[M1, k7, M1]**, k14, p2, k1, p1, k2.

Row 8: Sl 1, k1, p1, k1, p1, k1, p14, **[p9]**, p8, k1, p1, k1, p1, k2.

Row 9: Sl 1, k2tog, yo, k1, p2, k8, **[M1, k9, M1]**, k14, p2, k1, yo, k2tog, k1.

Row 10: Sl 1, k1, p1, k1, p1, k1, p14, **[p11]**, p8, k1, p1, k1, p1, k2.

Row 11: Sl 1, k1, p1, k1, p2, k8, **[M1, k11, M1]**, k14, p2, k1, p1, k2.

Row 12: Sl 1, k1, p1, k1, p1, k1, p14, **[p13]**, p8, k1, p1, k1, p1, k2.

Row 13: Sl 1, k1, p1, k1, p2, k8, **[M1, k13, M1]**, k14, p2, k1, p1, k2.

Row 14: Sl 1, k1, p1, k1, p1, k1, p14, **[p15]**, p8, k1, p1, k1, p1, k2.

Row 15: Sl 1, k2tog, yo, k1, p2, k8, **[M1, *k1, p1, repeat from * 6 more times, k1, M1]**, k14, p2, yo, k1, k2tog, k1.

Row 16: Sl 1, k1, p1, k1, p1, k1, p14, **[* p1, k1, repeat from * 7 more times, p1]**, p8, k1, p1, k1, p1, k2.

Row 17: Sl 1, k1, p1, k1, p2, k8, **[M1, *p 1, k1, repeat from * 7 more times, p1, M1]**, k14, p2, k1, p1, k2.

Row 18: Sl 1, k1, p1, k1, p1, k1, p14, (drop marker) **[BO 17 sts in seed st]**, (drop marker), p7, k1, p1, k1, p1, k2.

Row 19: Sl 1, k1, p1, k1, p2, k8, **[CO 3 sts]**, k14, p2, k1, p1, k2.

Row 20: Sl 1, k1, p1, k1, p1, k1, p25, k1, p1, k1, p1, k2.

HAND

Return to wrist pattern, **starting with Row 3.**

Finish out that 6-row set (3 additional rows).

Work one more full set (6 rows).

Work the first 3 rows of another set.

Work this row of seed stitch 4 times: Sl 1 *k 1, p1, repeat from to 2 sts from end, k2.

BO in pattern.

FINISHING

Spray or steam block both pieces, gently pulling borders to spread seed st and pinning at frequent intervals to make edges as straight as possible, and let dry. Blocked pieces should measure at least 6"/15cm wide.

Carefully lace satin ribbon through eyelets from top (thumb-side) to bottom, keeping it as flat as possible, tying with bow at bottom.

Criss-Cross Gloves Variation

For a luxury cold-weather version of the gloves, use 2 balls Knit Picks *Ambrosia* (50g; 110yd/100m; 80% baby alpaca, 20% cashmere), shown here in 23744 grass. Work on US 2 or 3 at 24 sts = 4"/10cm. Replace the 6-st side borders of seed st and eyelet with 7 sts of stockinette, and seam up the sides. Because they'll be seamed, you can save some brainpower and knit both at once, by centering the thumbs. Just center the bolded portion 18 sts in from either side, and work thumb as usual.

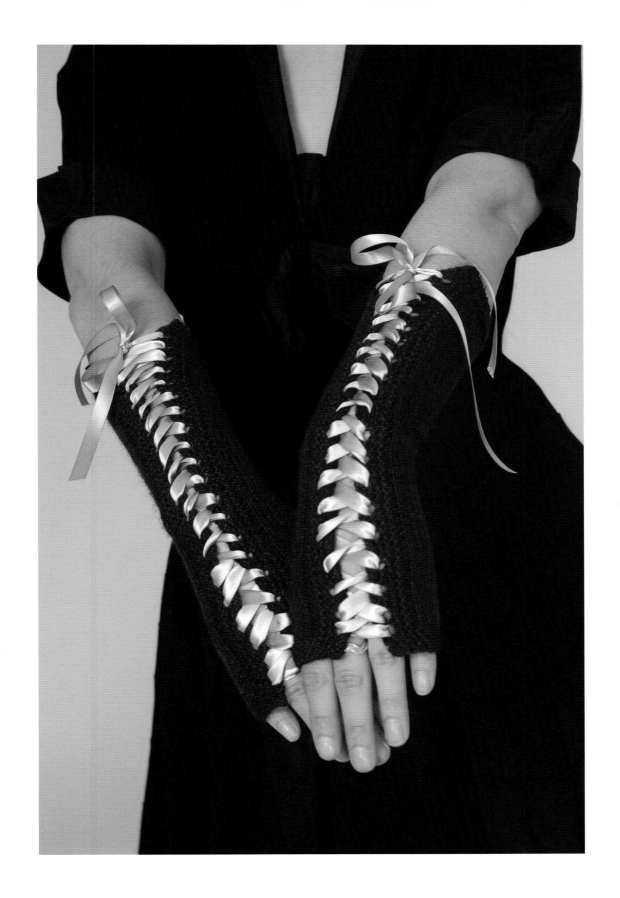

Garter

The garter shown is laced with wide ribbon through every other eyelet. Alternately, you could skip every other eyelet (substituting Row 5 for Row 3 in every other set), or use ⅜"/19mm ribbon and lace through every hole.

FRONT PANEL

CO (49, 63, 77, 91) sts.

UPPER EDGE

Work a seed st border, start eyelets:

Row 1 (RS) & 2 (WS): Sl 1, *k 1, p1, repeat from * to last 2 sts, k2.

Row 3: Sl 1, k2tog, yo, *k 1, p1, repeat from * to last 4 sts, k1, yo, k2tog, k1.

Row 4 & 5: Repeat Rows 1 & 2.

Place markers, work a seed st edge, knit WS main row to result in a RS purl border between seed st and stockinette st:

Row 6: Sl 1, k1, p1, k1, p1, k1, PM, k to 6 st from end, PM, k1, p1, k1, p1, k2.

HIP SHAPING

Row 1 (RS): Sl 1, k1, p1, k1, p2, SM, k1, M1, k to within 1 st of marker, M1, k1, p2, k1, p1, k2.

Row 2 (WS): Sl 1, k1, p1, k1, p1, k1, p to marker, k1, p1, k1, p1, k2.

Row 3: Sl 1, k2tog, yo, k1, p2, k to marker, p2, k1, yo, k2tog, k1.

Row 4: Row 2.

Row 5: Sl 1, k1, p1, k1, p2, k to marker, p2, k1, p1, k2.

Row 6: Repeat Row 2.

Repeat 6 rows 6 more times—63 (77, 91, 105) sts.

Then repeat set below until piece measures 6 (6, 7, 7)"/15 (15, 18, 18)cm.

Row 1 (RS): Sl 1, k1, p1, k1, p2, k to marker, p2, k1, p1, k2.

Row 2 (WS): Sl 1, k1, p1, k1, p1, k1, p to marker, k1, p1, k1, p1, k2.

Row 3: Sl 1, k2tog, yo, k1, p2, k to marker, p2, k1, yo, k2tog, k1.

Row 4: Repeat Row 2.

Row 5: Repeat Row 1.

Row 6: Repeat Row 2.

LOWER EDGE

Row 1 (RS): Sl 1, k1, p1, k1, p2, p to marker, p2, k1, p1, k2.

Row 2 (WS): Sl 1, *k 1, p1, repeat from * to last 2 sts, k2.

Repeat last row 6 more times, then BO in seed st.

BACK PANEL

CO 63 (77, 91, 105) sts.

Proceed exactly as for front.

Stitch count after hip shaping increase—77 (91, 105, 119) sts.

FINISHING

Steam or spray block both pieces, gently pulling borders to spread seed st and making edges as straight as possible, and let dry.

Find and mark center bottom of each piece.

Halfway between the center and the edge, pick up and knit 4 sts and knit 4 rows stockinette st and BO. Slip tab through garter st clip, fold under and sew down. Repeat for remaining 3 garter tabs.

Carefully lace satin ribbon through eyelets from top to bottom, keeping them as flat as possible, tying with bow at bottom.

GARTER
Back: block to 10½ (12½, 15, 17¼)"
Front: block to 8 (10½, 12½, 15)"

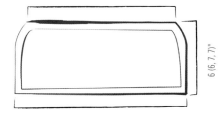

6 (6, 7, 7)"

Front: block to 10½ (12½, 15, 17¼)"
Back: block to 12½ (15, 17¼, 20)"

Mrs. Robinson

This sparkly bra has an opulence you may associate with a more sophisticated vixen. It's also so hot you'll want to eat yourself up with a spoon. Here's where a fancy yarn can really make a garment sizzle. Karabella's Sequins is a lace mohair yarn strung with delicate, minute sequins, for gorgeous sparkle and feathery lightness. And even the XL uses only one ball, making the splurge quite agreeable.

SIZING
Women's S (M, L, XL)

YARN, ETC.
1 spool Karabella *Sequins* (108yd/99m; mohair with sequins), red (A)

1 ball Karabella *Empire Silk* (50g; 90yd/82m; 100% Italian silk), 503 red (or about 3yd/2.7m $\frac{1}{16}$–$\frac{1}{8}$"/1.5m–3mm wide red satin ribbon) (B)

2 yd/2m $\frac{5}{8}$"/1.6cm red satin ribbon

Red sewing thread

NEEDLES & NOTIONS
US 3/3.25mm circular (24"/61cm max), or for gauge

US 7/4.5mm needles

Sewing needle

Fray Check

GAUGE
Stockinette st, A: 23 sts = 4"/10cm

INSTRUCTIONS

LEFT CUP

You'll work in stockinette stitch with a slipped-stitch garter stitch border along one side (slipping the first and knitting 2 stitches at the beginning of all purled rows), working all decreases (always on even/purled rows) inside that garter stitch border.

Odd (RS/knit) rows: Sl 1, k to end.
Plain even (WS/purled) rows: Sl 1, k2, p to 1 st from end, k1.
Decreased even (WS/purled) rows: Sl 1, k2tog, k1, p to 1 st from end, k1.

With A, CO 18 (22, 26, 30) sts.

Knit 11 rows in stockinette st with slipped-stitch garter st border outlined above.

Row 12: Sl 1, k2tog, k1, p to 1 st from end, k1.

Decrease every 4th row (every other even row) until you have 13 (16, 19, 22) sts.

BUST DART

Without turning your work, examine the slipped-stitch border that goes down from your work at a right angle. Notice how the edge is made up of little chain links. Pick up and knit 1 st through the *far side only* of each chain (instead of going through both, as you normally might). This first row will be a little tight on your needles, but it will slack up as you work away from the dart.

Maintain garter st border, decrease as before every 4th row (every other even row), until you have worked 3 (3, 4, 4) decreases, or 12 (12, 16, 16) rows.

Work even, maintaining border, 6 (10, 10, 14) more rows.

Always slipping first and knitting last st, work 3 rows in k1, p1 rib.

BO in pattern.

RIGHT CUP

The right cup is worked from the WS in reverse stockinette stitch. The decreases are on the knit side, which means you're not dealing with the garter stitch border and a decrease at the same time.

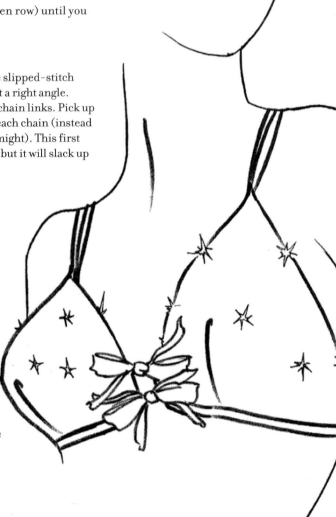

Odd (WS/purled) rows: Sl 1, p to 3 sts from end, k to end.
Plain even (RS/knit) rows: Sl 1, k to end.
Decreased even (RS/knit) rows: Sl 1, k2tog, k to end.

With A, CO 18 (22, 26, 30) sts.

Knit 11 rows in stockinette st with slipped-stitch garter st border.

Row 12: Sl 1, k2tog to 1 st from end, k1.

Decrease every 4th row (every other even row) until you have 13 (16, 19, 22) sts.

BUST DART

At the end of the decrease row that brings you to the above st, without turning your work, examine the slipped-st border. This time, pick up and knit 1 st through *both sides* of each chain. This first row will be a little tight on your needles, but it will slack up as you work away from the dart.

Continue to maintain that outer garter st border and decrease as before every 4th row (every other even row), until you have worked 3 (3, 4, 4) decreases, or 12 (12, 16, 16) rows.

Work even, maintaining border 6 (10, 10, 14) more rows.

Always slipping first and knitting last st, work 3 rows in k1, p1 rib.

BO in pattern.

BAND

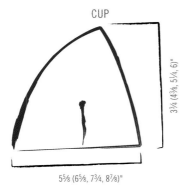

CUP

3¾ (4⅜, 5¼, 6)"

5⅝ (6⅝, 7¾, 8⅞)"

You'll either need a friend or a marker for this part, as the band must be knit to your size.

If you have a helper: Hold the cups, slightly stretched, over your breasts. Have your friend measure across your back, from bottom outside cup corner to bottom outside cup corner.

If you're on your own: Hold one cup, slightly stretched, over one breast, and mark where the bottom outer edge hits on your body. Mark the other cup the same way. Using a measuring tape around your back, measure from mark to mark.

With RS of cups facing, starting at bottom edge of left cup, pick up and knit 1 st into every other st until you hit the dart. Then pick up one st for each st until the end of the cup.

Now cast on 4 st for every inch of the measurement you just took (these sts will be stretched in wearing, so use fewer per inch than the cup gauge to keep it snug).

Then pick up sts along the bottom of the second cup (1 st per chain up to the dart, then 1 st for every other st presented to the end).

Work 1 row in k1, p1 rib, 3 rows stockinette st, and BO in k1, p1 rib. There should be 4 strands between the top and the back. Knot the ends together loosely, and pull top and strap apart gently. Try on the bra and adjust knot to fit.

STRAPS

Close the front with two 18"/45cm lengths of wider satin ribbon, tied into bows (simply weave the ribbon through the knitting).

Holding the top of the cup firmly, measure from the top of the cup down to the bra strap. If you don't have a helper, simply pin the end of your measuring tape to the strap before trying on the bra, then pull it over your shoulder and measure where it hits the top of the bra.

Measure and mark 2½" (6.5cm) out of center back of the bra strap.

For each shoulder strap, cut a length of B (or thin satin ribbon) 4 times the measurement you took above + 3"/7.5cm. Using a yarn needle, loop the yarn through the top of the cup and the top of the bra strap edge at marker, twice.

After you've fitted the strap, readjust the yarn or ribbon so that the knotted end is flush with the back strap. Trim down to ¼"/6.3mm and seal ends with Fray Check. Let dry completely (takes an hour or so), then tack down ends to the inside of the bra strap using sewing thread.

Hootchie
Kootchie

I wish I had the confidence to perform a good old-fashioned bump and grind, if only for my own mirror. I always strive for a picture I once saw of Lili St. Cyr. She was barefoot, low to the ground, and grinding; tossing her hair and smiling the wild, laughing smile of someone having a ball. But whenever I try (alone, of course, with door locked, but still embarrassed and looking over my shoulder), it always seems weird and phony, like TV strippers, or really funny and a little creepy, like a six-year-old girl shaking her ass to provocative pop song.

But that's just because I didn't have the right outfit. With my sparkly new pasties, I'll be Lili-freaking-St. Cyr before you know it.

1½ (2, 2½, 3, 3½)"/3.8 (5, 6.5, 7.5, 9)cm
diameter

Where no parentheses are used, instructions/
quantities apply to all sizes

YARN
1 ball Lion Brand *Glitterspun* (50g; 115yd/105m;
60% acrylic, 27% Cupro, 13% Polyester), color of
your choice* (A)

*or use about 20 yds (18m) of any glam leftovers
from your stash that work at the same gauge

OPTIONAL:
1 ball Berroco *Laser FX* (10g; 70yd/64m; 100%
polyester with sequins), color of your choice (B)

NEEDLES & NOTIONS
US 4 (3.5mm) double-pointed needles, or close
size (gauge not too critical)

GAUGE
ALWAYS CHECK YOUR GAUGE! Measure
unwashed and unblocked, just relaxed and patted
flat (NOT smoothed out)

Stockinette st, A: 24 sts = 4"/10cm

INSTRUCTIONS

1½ (2, 2½, 3, 3½)"

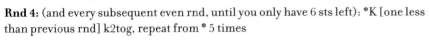

The pasties are knit in a jiffy in the round on double-pointed needles; they're a fast and low-pain introduction to dpns.

To go larger than the listed sizes, increase CO sts in increments of 6. To arrive at that first number of stitches knit before the decrease (the first part of Row 2), simply divide your CO number by 6 and subtract 2.

With A (and B, if you like), CO 24 (30, 42, 54, 66) sts. Divide between 3 dpns and join, being careful not to twist stitches.

Rnd 1: *K 1, p1, repeat from * to end.

Rnd 2: *K2 (3, 5, 7, 9), k2tog, repeat from * 5 more times—18 (24, 36, 48) sts.

Rnd 3: (and every odd rnd): Knit.

Rnd 4: (and every subsequent even rnd, until you only have 6 sts left): *K [one less than previous rnd] k2tog, repeat from * 5 times

Continue in this manner, working in sets of 6 and knitting fewer stitches before the k2tog in each set, until you finally have only 6 sts left on your needles. Cut the yarn, leaving an 8"/20cm tail. Using a yarn needle, run the tail through all the live sts, slipping them off their needles. Pass needle through, stitch tail down to underside, weave in, and trim as you like.

Repeat with mate.

Apply with false-eyelash glue. (For best results, coat the outer edge and spiral in, spread thinly, then let dry for about 30 seconds, until tacky, before applying).

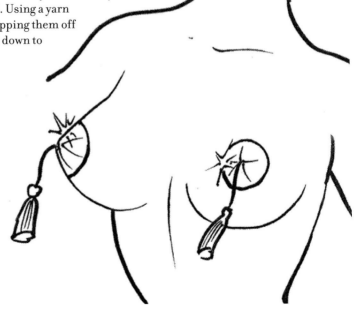

Bound and Determined

HOMEMADE BONDAGE gear is nothing new. Industrious dilettantes have long fashioned restraints on the fly from whatever's been handy. But the idea of applying traditional crafts, the stuff of *Workbasket* and *Better Homes and Gardens* and even *Martha Stewart Living*, to bondage clothing and accessories, made me positively giddy. These projects are as fun as they are functional—or, as fun as they are impractical, depending on your tastes. The point is: they're fun.

The smaller accessories are quick to knit and surprisingly darling, considering. Usually ball gags are menacing, but knit out of colorful acrylic grandma yarn, they're downright cute. And with build-it-yourself bondage, you get more than basic black and red. Now you can finally make a flogger to match your curtains, hurrah!

And you can turn up the fun dial even higher by customizing the patterns for a craftier feel. If you think a Baby Blue Ball Gag is too sinister, why not add a row of Fair Isle duckies all around or embroider on a happy face? Or work a duplicate stitch QUIET TIME across the front of your ball gag. But watch out—you might find that the more grandma/Hobby Lobby you get, the creepier things become.

If discipline and restraint don't suit you, there's a straight version of the straitjacket; and the corset looks equally fetching as outerwear, either over a dress or under a suit jacket. Plus, there's always Halloween. Even my mom (see Mrs. Robinson, p.80) was a dominatrix for Halloween—she was a smash hit, not surprisingly.

Or maybe you'd like to get your feet wet before investing in a big project. I once had a boyfriend who begged me and begged me to tie him up. When I finally agreed, he immediately had a panic attack and hyperventilated and I had to race to get the knots out. You wouldn't want to knit yourself a straitjacket sweater and find out afterwards you're him. If you're not sure, start small. Grab something bulky from your stash and start a 5-stitch I-cord, and don't stop until you're out of yarn. You'll have a nice, sturdy (and fashionable!) rope for a little practice run. If it doesn't work out, you can always use it to tie down all those boxes on your next trip to IKEA.

. . . The idea of applying traditional crafts to bondage gear made me positively giddy.

Felt Up

This quick-knit beauty is first knit to fit and then felted several inches narrower for a stiff body and snug lacing. The corset panels are knit sideways and shaped with short rows. The garter stitch edges, seamed together, give a boned effect when felted. A wool-blend yarn facilitates lazy machine felting, and the non-felted portions create an unusual, nubby tweed effect.

SIZING

Women's S (M, L, XL)

Where no parentheses are used, instructions/quantities apply to all sizes

YARN, ETC.

4 (5, 6, 7) balls Lion Brand *Landscapes* (50g; 55yd/50m; 50% wool, 50% acrylic), 279 deep sea

5 yd/4.5m 100% cotton waste yarn

6 yd/5.4m red satin ribbon (width to suit you: ⅝"/16mm to 1⅛"/2.8cm)

NEEDLES & NOTIONS

US 13/9mm needles, or for gauge

Safety pins

Stainless steel T pins

Large cork board, blocking board, or an ironing board you won't need for a few days

Bath towels

Spray bottle or washcloth

US 7/4.5mm or close knitting needle

A large cork board (used horizontally) is a great, inexpensive knitting notion. It's outstanding for felting, when you might need a little extra resistance reshaping edges, but it's also very handy for any blocking, and having a firm, broad, portable surface means you can whisk projects out of the way while they're drying without the risk of distorting their shape.

GAUGE

ALWAYS CHECK YOUR GAUGE!

Before felting: Stockinette st: 9½ sts and 13 rows = 4"/10cm

After felting: About 12 sts and 19 rows (slight variation is OK)

INSTRUCTIONS

A "short row" is a row that's worked only partially, before it's turned, and worked in the opposite direction. We'll use them here to make the side and front panels flare out a bit at the top and bottom while maintaining a slender middle. If you're unfamiliar with short row shaping, short row wraps, or knitting in wraps, or if you need a refresher course, review the "Techniques" section (p. 133) and make a couple of swatches so you feel comfortable.

You'll be knitting each panel sideways. The top and bottom of your work will later become the side seams of the corset, and your sides the top and bottom edges of your corset.

The corset falls halfway down the hips, so it's not a true hourglass—⅔ of the corset is above the waist and ⅓ is below. Consequently, your boobs are more critical than your hips in choosing a size. Go down a size if you're unsure.

BACK PANEL 1 (RIGHT WHEN FLAT, LEFT WHEN WORN)

CO 34 sts.

Knit 2 rows.

Row 3 (RS): K1, *k2tog, yo, k2, repeat from * to 1 st from edge, k1.

Knit 2 rows.

Work 6 (6, 10, 10) rows in stockinette st, starting with a purled row and ending with a knit row.

Knit 2 rows.

BO all sts.

With RS facing, examine eyelet row. The side with 3 sts after the last eyelet is the bottom, and the side with 2 stitches is the top. Mark the top with a safety pin.

BACK PANEL 2 (LEFT WHEN FLAT, RIGHT WHEN WORN)

Just as Back Panel 1, except Row 3:

Row 3 (RS): K2, *k2tog, yo, k2, repeat from * to end.

Again, the side with 3 stitches after the last eyelet is the bottom, and the side with 2 stitches is the top. Mark the top with a safety pin.

SIDE PANELS (KNIT 2)

CO 34 sts.

K3 rows.

Starting with WS (P), work 3 rows stockinette st.

K16, wrap and turn (first bust short row).

P to edge.

K across entire row, catching and knitting in 1 wrap.

P8, wrap and turn (first hip short row).

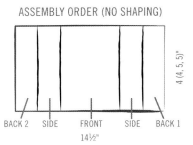

ASSEMBLY ORDER (NO SHAPING)

BACK 2   SIDE   FRONT   SIDE   BACK 1

14½"

4 (4, 5, 5)"

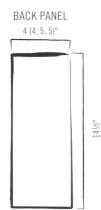

BACK PANEL

4 (4, 5, 5)"

14½"

K to edge.

P across entire row, catching and purling in 1 wrap.

Starting with RS (K) row, work 0 (0, 4, 4) rows stockinette st.

K16, wrap and turn (second bust short row).

P to edge.

K across entire row, catching and knitting in 1 wrap.

P8, wrap and turn (second hip short row).

K to edge.

P across entire row, catching and purling in 1 wrap.

Starting with RS (K), work 3 rows stockinette st.

K2 rows.

BO all sts.

The pinched-in portion is off center. In relation to the narrow portion, there's one long flared side (with bust short rows) and one short flared side (with hip short rows). Mark the edge of the longer side of each panel with a safety pin.

FRONT PANEL

The front is knit in the opposite direction to the side panels, so the bust short rows are purled and the hip short rows are knit. This panel has 3 multirow short row clusters at each end.

CO 34 sts.

K3 rows.

Starting with WS (P), work 3 (5, 7, 7) rows stockinette st.

P16, wrap and turn (bust short row).

K to edge.

P12, wrap and turn (bust short row).

K to edge.

P across full row, catching and purling in 2 wraps.

K8, wrap and turn (hip short row).

P to edge.

K5, wrap and turn (hip short row).

P to edge.

K across full row, catching and knitting in 2 wraps.

Starting with WS (P), work 2 (4, 4, 6) rows stockinette st.

P16, wrap and turn (bust short row).

K to edge.

P12, wrap and turn (bust short row).

K to edge.

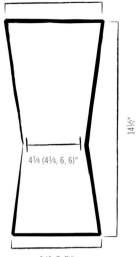

SIDE PANEL (MAKE 2)

6 (6, 7, 7)"

14½"

4¾ (4¾, 6, 6)"

6 (6, 7, 7)"

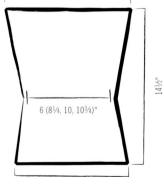

FRONT PANEL

10 (12½, 14⅜, 15)"

14½"

6 (8¼, 10, 10¾)"

10 (12½, 14⅜, 15)"

P18, wrap and turn (bust short row), catching and purling in 2 wraps.

K to edge.

P across full row, catching and purling in 1 wrap.

K8, wrap and turn (hip short row).

P to edge.

K6, wrap and turn (hip short row).

P to edge.

K4, wrap and turn (hip short row).

P to edge.

K across full row, catching and knitting in 3 wraps.

Starting with WS (p) and ending with k row, work 2 (4, 4, 6) rows stockinette st.

P16, wrap and turn (bust short row).

K to edge.

P12, wrap and turn (bust short row).

K to edge.

P across full row, catching and purling in 2 wraps.

K8, wrap and turn (hip short row).

P to edge.

K5, wrap and turn (hip short row).

P to edge.

K across full row, catching and knitting in 2 wraps.

Starting with WS (P) row, work 2 (4, 6, 6) rows stockinette st.

K2 rows.

BO all sts.

Again, there will be one long flared side (with bust short rows) and one short flared side (with hip short rows). Mark the edge of the longer side of the panel with a safety pin.

SEAMING AND EDGING

Working on a flat surface, with the panels sideways (CO/BO edges vertical), and all the safety pinned edges at the top, arrange the panels in order: back panel with eyelets on the left, side panel, front panel, side panel, back panel with eyelets on the right.

Working flat, seam panels with a running st that goes back and forth through CO/BO edges. This keeps the garter ridge edges prominent instead of hiding them in a seam.

EDGE TOP AND BOTTOM

With RS facing, pick up all sts along top of corset, then turn and BO all sts.

Repeat along bottom edge.

Weave in just an inch or so of all ends. You want to minimize bulk, which is accentuated in felting.

FELTING

Baste a double or triple strand of cotton yarn loosely through all the eyelets to keep them open in felting.

With hottest water and a few spoonfuls of dish soap, plus a couple of pairs of jeans, felt corset in the washing machine. Check progress at the end of the wash cycle. The fabric should be very dense and the sts indistinct, with bright bumps of color popping through the felt throughout (that's the acrylic fiber). You might need to run it through a second wash cycle.

After about 30 seconds of the spin cycle (just enough to get the bulk of the water out), remove it from the machine and roll it up in a towel and press to remove the rest of the water. The spin cycle can cause hard creasing. (If you forget to take it out in time, don't despair—you can rewet and tug the creases out, but it's a lot of work.)

BLOCKING

The corset is 3-dimensional, so it's a little tricky to block. After smoothing out all the edges, you'll block the corset in 2 steps. First you'll block the front and back panels, pinning them firmly to the board to make the edges nice and straight. After it dries completely, you'll rewet the top and bottom edges of just the side panels and block those separately. I like to block on a large cork board, but you can use an ironing board with a dry towel pinned around it instead.

The wool blend bunches a lot less than pure wool, so smoothing the edges shouldn't be too much work. Firmly tug top and bottom edges all along corset to smooth. If you hit an irregular spot along the edge, hold the edge firmly an inch or two down and tug with the other hand to even it out.

Holding at back panel, tug back edges firmly to smooth. Remove the cotton waste yarn and work your fingers into the eyelets to spread them open.

Start with the front panel, pinning it to your blocking surface firmly at the top and bottom edges to make them perfectly straight and parallel to each other.

With the side panels slack, pin the edges of the back panels to the board along the tops and edges, making the edges nice and straight.

If you're satisfied with the edges along the side panel, you can skip the next step.

After the corset is completely dry (may take a day or so), rewet the top and bottom edges of the side panels only (using a spray bottle or a water saturated washcloth) and block them nice and straight.

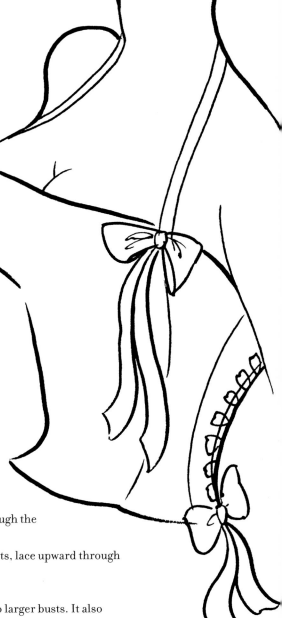

FINISHING

The corset must be utterly dry. If not, it will stretch and distort. We'll lace the corset at both ends, starting with the waist-level eyelets, so it can be tightened in both directions.

FOR THE LACES
Cut the ribbon into three 2 yd/2m lengths.

Starting with the third eyelets from the bottom, lace downward through the bottom 3 pairs (so it will tie at the bottom).

With the second piece of ribbon, starting with the same pair of eyelets, lace upward through the top 6 pairs (so it will tie at the top).

FOR THE NECK STRAP
The neck strap is optional for smaller breasts, but gives a great lift to larger busts. It also makes a pretty frame around the cleavage and neckline.

With the corset on and laced and centered, stand up straight. With the opposite arm handing slack, pin the top edge about 2"/5cm from the armpit on either side. Make sure both marks are symmetrical in relation to the front panel. Using a US 7 (or close) knitting needle, work a hole into the fabric about an inch down from marked spot.

Cut the end of the remaining ribbon at a sharp angle and feed through one of the holes, around your neck, and through the other hole. Bring the end back over your neck and tie the ends in a bow, which can be left near the edge or moved to the back.

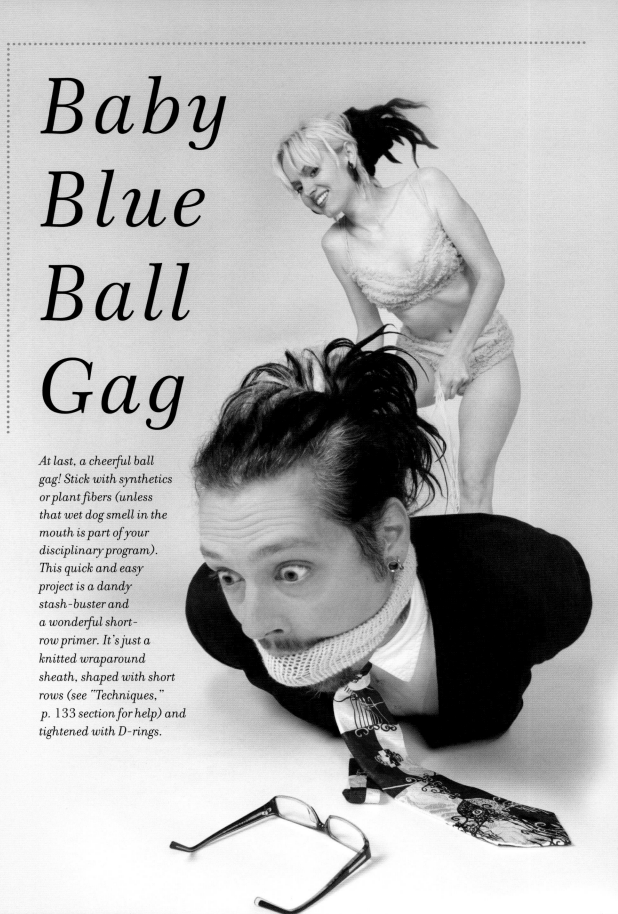

Baby Blue Ball Gag

At last, a cheerful ball gag! Stick with synthetics or plant fibers (unless that wet dog smell in the mouth is part of your disciplinary program). This quick and easy project is a dandy stash-buster and a wonderful short-row primer. It's just a knitted wraparound sheath, shaped with short rows (see "Techniques," p. 133 section for help) and tightened with D-rings.

INSTRUCTIONS

This uses a 2"/5cm hard rubber ball (look in the pet department), but it will work with smaller (foam practice golf balls) or larger (raquetballs) ones as well. The open back allows you to pop out the ball for washing (or switching sizes) in a snap.

YARN, ETC.
50g of worsted or sport weight yarn of your choice, preferably synthetic or plant fibers

2¾ D-rings

2"/5cm hard rubber ball

NEEDLES & NOTIONS
US 8/5mm needles, or for gauge

GAUGE
ALWAYS CHECK YOUR GAUGE!
Measure unwashed and unblocked, just relaxed and patted flat (NOT smoothed out)

Stockinette st (single strand of worsted; double strand of sport weight): 19 sts = 4"/10cm

CO 90 sts.

Purl.

Knit.

P70, wrap & turn.

K50, wrap & turn.

P45, wrap & turn.

K40, wrap & turn.

P35, wrap & turn.

K30, wrap & turn.

P25, wrap & turn.

K20, wrap & turn.

P15, wrap & turn.

K10, wrap & turn.

P40, (catch 5 wraps) wrap & turn.

K70, (catch 5 wraps) wrap & turn.

P65, wrap& turn.

K60, wrap & turn.

P55, wrap & turn.

K50, wrap & turn.

P45, wrap & turn.

K40, wrap & turn.

P35, wrap & turn.

K30, wrap & turn.

P25, wrap & turn.

K20, wrap& turn.

P to end (catch 6 wraps).

K to end (catch 7 wraps).

P80, wrap & turn.

K70, wrap & turn.

P65, wrap & turn.

K60, wrap & turn.

P55, wrap & turn.

K50, wrap & turn.

P45, wrap & turn.

K40, wrap & turn.

P35, wrap & turn.

K30, wrap & turn.

P25, wrap & turn.

K20, wrap & turn.

P15, wrap & turn.

K10, wrap & turn.

P to end (catch 5 wraps).

K to end (catch 6 wraps).

BO all sts.

FINISHING

Block piece flat.

Overlap and seam ends up 4"/10cm in on either side.

Slip one end through D-rings, fold over, and seam.

Weave in yarn ends.

Slip ball into sheath for use.

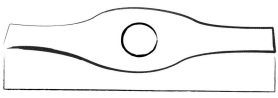

19"

Straitjacket

Today's modern sociopath deserves a straitjacket that is as attractive as she is. This collarless body-hugging raglan pullover has extralong sleeves that cross in front and clink together with spring-clip hardware in back. The sleeves feature dropped-stitch ladders that show off both skin and yarn texture and delight with their get-nervous vibe. The shaping comes from side ribs, not increases and decreases, thus making the style equally suitable for a man (though the sleeve ladders do demand a daring man). I've used bruise-colored thick-and-thin faux-handspun wool. If you're a traditionalist, use a cotton or cotton-blend yarn instead. Try 10 (12, 14, 16) balls Reynolds Cabana (100g; 135yd/123m; 65% cotton, 35% acrylic) in 904 natural, doubled, for a refined finish, or 2 (3, 3, 4) skeins Henry's Attic Inca Cotton (8oz; 325yd; 100% organic cotton), doubled, for a more rustic look. And if you think Lunatic Asylum chic is totally last year, you can knit it civilian, with shorter sleeves and no tell-tale hardware.

SIZING
Women's S (M, L, XL)

Where no parentheses are used, instructions/quantities apply to all sizes

YARN, ETC.
5 (6, 7, 8) hanks Berroco *Hip Hop* (100g; 76yd/70m, 100% wool), 7240 zion

1 similarly sized D-ring
1 swivelling metal spring clip

NEEDLES & NOTIONS
US 13/9mm needles, or for gauge

US 11/8mm needles (or 1 size down from larger size)

GAUGE
ALWAYS CHECK YOUR GAUGE!
Measure unwashed and unblocked, just relaxed and patted flat (NOT smoothed out).

Stockinette st on larger needles:
9 sts and 12 sts = 4"/10cm

INSTRUCTIONS

If you're sensitive, *Hip-Hop* can be a bit coarse against the skin, but it does soften (both in touch and appearance) with washing. Use cold water and a light hand to prevent fibers from felting. I like to use a gentle shampoo and apply a bit of hair conditioner in the rinse for added softness. Roll out excess water, pat into shape, and dry flat.

FRONT AND BACK (KNIT 2)

With smaller needles, CO 31 (35, 39, 43) sts.

Work 4 rows in k1, p1 rib.

Switch to larger needles.

Now you'll work in stockinette stitch flanked with 6 (6, 8, 8) sts of k1, p1 rib on either side. Use markers to flag where the ribbing ends/begins.

[K1, P1] 3 (3, 4, 4) times, PM, k19 (23, 23, 27), PM, [p1, k1] 3 (3, 4, 4) times.

Work in pattern until piece measures 14 (15, 16, 17)"/36 (38, 41, 43)cm, ending with WS row.

ARMHOLES

To keep the edges distinct for seaming, work 3 sts in from each side: K3, ssk, k to 5 st from end, k2tog k3.

BO 4 (4, 5, 5) sts in pattern at the beg of next 2 rows. After binding off, you'll ignore the remaining st or two of that rib pattern and work in plain stockinette.

Dec 1 st each side every RS row, a total 5 (5, 6, 6) times. Purl WS rows.

After working specified decrease rows, complete WS row, and BO remaining sts knitwise.

SLEEVES (KNIT 2)

Most of the sleeve shaping won't happen until the very end, when you form the ladders. The straightened yarn rungs that result when you drop the stitches will take up considerably more space than their equivalent stitches, effectively increasing your overall sleeve width without requiring many knitted increases.

With smaller needles, CO 23 (23, 27, 27) sts.

Work in k1, p1 rib for 14 (14, 15, 15)"/35.5 (35.5, 38, 38)cm. (This might not seem long enough for clipping behind the back, but the sleeves are stretchy, and you don't want your straitjacket too loose.)

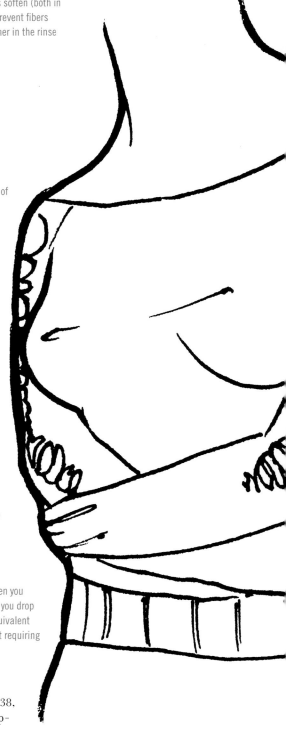

SHAPE SLEEVE

Switch to larger needles and work in stockinette st from here on. In a few rows, you'll place markers and insert the stitches that will become the dropped stitch ladder. From that row on, twist every stitch before the first marker and every stitch after the second maker on every RS row. This firms up the sts on either side of the to-be-dropped sts, keeping everything tidy later on.

Work 6 rows in stockinette.

Row 7: K11 (11, 13, 13), k1tbl, PM, yo, PM, k1tbl, k to end. The big ugly yo holes will vanish into the ladder when you drop those stitches later on.

Row 8: P all stitches, including yo—24 (24, 28, 28) sts.

Rows 9–16: Work in stockinette st.

Row 17: K11 (11, 13, 13) k1tbl, k1 yo, k1tbl, k to end.

Row 18: P all stitches, including yo—25 (25, 29, 29) sts.

Continue in stockinette st until piece measures 26 (26, 27, 27)"/66 (66, 68.5, 68.5)cm, ending with WS row.

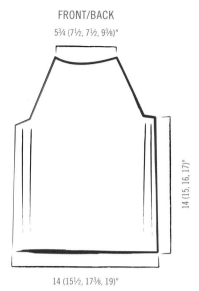

FRONT/BACK

5¾ (7½, 7½, 9⅜)"

14 (15, 16, 17)"

14 (15½, 17⅜, 19)"

SHAPE CAP

There's not room to work 3 sts in from the edge on the sleeves as you did on the torso, but do place your decreases 2 sts in for as long as you can (you'll have to fudge on the far end of your last decrease row, as that half has fewer sts). Also, maintain that twisted (ktbl) st on either side of the center ladder-to-be for as long as you can.

BO 4 (4, 5, 5) sts at beg of next 2 rows.

Dec 1 st each side every RS row 5 (5, 6, 6) times.

To keep track of it all, I've outlined every decrease row. The first row shown is an extra row for L and XL sizes only. After that, all 4 sizes are worked the same.

FOR L/XL ONLY (S/M: SKIP TO ALL SIZES)

K2, ssk, k4, k1tbl, k2, k1tbl, k3, k2tog, k2.

P1 row. From here, all sizes decrease the same.

ALL SIZES

K2, ssk, k3, k1tbl, k2, k1tbl, k2, k2tog, k2.

P1 row.

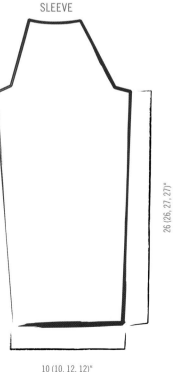

SLEEVE

26 (26, 27, 27)"

10 (10, 12, 12)"

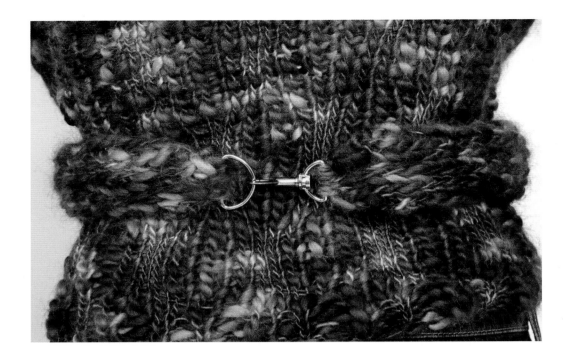

K2, ssk, k2, k1tbl, k2, k1tbl, k1, k2tog, k2.

P1 row.

K2, ssk, k1, k1tbl, k2, k1tbl, k2tog, K2.

P1 row.

K2, ssk, k1tbl, k2, k2tog tbl, k2.

P row.

K2, ssk, k2, k2tog tbl, k1.

P1 row.

BO 3 sts. *Yo, draw through live st (binding it off), repeat from * 7 more times, drop next 2 sts, BO to end.

With your fingers and/or your needle, work out those dropped sts all the way down, into a nice ladder. The wool can be sticky, so make sure you don't lose track of a st halfway down. You'll be unraveling 2 sts most of the way down. The bottom quarter or so of the ladder will be just one st, which creates a nice taper.

FINISHING

You can also control the shape an awful lot by blocking, so if you want changes to length or width, shape the garment and block it more sternly before letting it dry.

Block all pieces.

Seam shoulders

Seam sleeves and sides, working out from armpits.

Seam open ends of sleeves and sew swivel spring clip to one sleeve and D-ring to other.

Alternately, leave the sleeve ends open and sew hardware to open sleeve edges. Then you can cuff the straightjacket sleeves when you wish, hiding your hardware.

Weave in all ends.

Strap Happy (Fun with Leftover Yarn & Hardware)

Once I got started with D-rings, I just couldn't stop. There's something so satisfying about an adjustable strap!

Here are six dandy projects you can make with stuff from your stash, or leftover yarn from the projects in this book (listed by pattern and yarn). They're fast, nearly free (you already have the yarn, and the hardware is around a buck) and double-plus fun. If you're not a free former by nature, you can find simple patterns for all of these ideas and pictures, plus instructions for casting on around a D-ring, at naughtyneedlesknitting.com.

SEXY CHOKER
(JEWELRY FINDINGS + DELICATE/GLITZY YARN)
Fembot (*Kid Merino, Gossamer, Prima*), Mrs. Robinson (*Sequins*), Bond Girl/Goldfinger (*Glitterspun, Brilliant*), Zelda (*Breeze*), Criss-Cross (*Alpaca Silk*).

FELTED CUFFS
(PLAIN OR RHINESTONE D-RINGS + ANIMAL FIBERS)
Kinderwhore or Arrgh! (*Sport Weight 100% Alpaca*), Felt Up (*Landscapes*), Nursie (*Decadence*), Into the Woods (*Bulky Hand Dyes*), Straitjacket (*Hip-Hop*).

PLUSH EAR WARMER HEADBAND
(LARGE D-RINGS + WARM OR CUDDLY YARN)
Ice Vixen (*Softy*), Siren (various), Nursie (*Decadence*).

BELT
(LARGE D- OR O-RINGS + LOW-STRETCH YARN)
Mrs. Robinson (*Empire Silk*), Zelda (*Breeze*), Disobey Madame (*Leather/Suede Lace*), Fish Net (*Optik*), or any of the felted cuff choices (felted).

COZY CHOKER SCARF
(LARGE D-RINGS + PLUSHY YARN/S)
(*Bonus: Uses half the yarn of a regular scarf!*) Kinderwhore (*Sport Weight 100% Alpaca*), Dirty Secrets and Condom Critters (*Hello Yarn/Maisy Day Handspun*), Ice Vixen (*Softy*), Criss-Cross Variation (*Ambrosia*), Felt Up (*Landscapes*), Siren (various plush).

HOT JAVA/COLD BEER SNUGGLER
(2 SETS SMALL D-RINGS + ANIMAL FIBERS)
Any of the felted cuff choices.

Sweater Variation

If you're no longer a danger to yourself or others, you may knit the *compos mentis* version.

The only change you'll make is the sleeve:

Work the k1, p1 ribbing for 8 (8, 9, 9)"/20.5 (20.5, 23, 23)cm instead of 14/15"/35.5/38cm

The total before shaping the cap will measure 21 (21, 22, 22)"/53.5 (53.5, 56, 56)cm instead of 30/31"/76/79cm.

And, of course, you'll leave off the hardware.

Disobey Madame At Your Peril

Years ago, I scored a pile of dominatrix business/ad cards in a London phone booth. I was utterly delighted that the notorious English naughty schoolboy stereotype was real enough to warrant phone booths getting positively shingled in these hilarious cards. My favorites warned DISOBEY MADAME AT YOUR PERIL, ARROGANT BOY REDUCED TO TEARS, and IF IT'S PAIN YOU WANT, IT'S AGONY YOU'LL GET! So much better than my business cards.

If you never venture out of the yarn store for your knitting, it's time to start. Suede and leather lacing are surprisingly inexpensive (under $10 for 25 yd) and available in a nice array of colors. If leather's not your bag, critter-free alternatives (plastic lanyard, rubber necklace cord, or heavy twine) abound. Best of all, they can be finished in about an hour.

Thwack!

Suede lacing comes in more than a dozen colors, so you can knit a rainbow. Inspired by the vegan-friendly rubber flogger made by my friend Rubber Jen, this can just as easily be knit of vinyl lanyard, rubber jewelry cord, or a triple thickness of metallic cord (like Lion Brand Lame; 19g; 75yd/67m; 65% rayon, 35% metalized polyester).

YARN, ETC.
1 spool Tejas Lace Company *Suede Lace* (⅛" x 25yd; 100% suede leather), 07 red (available at craft stores, see "Resources," p. 141)
Small zip ties, clear or red (available at general merchandise, hardware or electronics stores)

NEEDLES & NOTIONS
US 15/10mm needles, or comfortable size
Large crochet hook

GAUGE
Gauge is not critical

about 6"

about 15"

INSTRUCTIONS

Cut six 2-yd/2m lengths of suede.

Holding them bunched together, flush at one end, zip tie bundle and loosely braid 12"/30cm.

Loop braid to form a strap and zip tie it off. Several feet of cord will remain.

Take the loose end of the bundle and fold it in half, in towards just under where the braid is tied. Zip tie it into the bundle.

Then take the far looped end and slip a zip tie through all the loops so they're held together.

Now fold the zipped, looped end back in towards the braid as well. This results in a double loop of suede, or 4 times the original volume.

Fasten down securely with zip ties. Trim all zip tie ends.

HANDLE WRAP

Leaving an 18"/46cm tail, CO 6 sts.

Work 3 rows in garter st.

Work 10 rows of stockinette st.

Work 3 more rows of garter st.

BO all sts.

The natural curl of the stockinette will make shaping the handle around flogger easy. Wrap around zip-tied center to conceal all ties. Seam from the bottom up, and then weave in end down through shaft and out bottom (feed a crochet hook up through the center and drag the end down). Trim off to match length.

Kitten with a Whip

This snaky, flexible leather whip has a rubber grip.

YARN, ETC.

1 spool Tejas Lace Company *Round Leather Lace* (2mm x 25yd; 100% leather), 01 black (available at craft stores, see "Resources," p. 140)
Small zip ties, clear or black (available at general merchandise, hardware or electronics stores)
One 4–5"/10–13cm piece black rubber hose (similar to garden hose; sold by the foot at hardware stores)

NEEDLES AND NOTIONS

US 5/3.75mm metal double-pointed needles, or comfortable size
H crochet hook, or close size

GAUGE

Gauge is not critical

I-CORD KITTEN NOTES

Metal double-pointed needles work best here.

Knit as loosely as possible, tugging each new stitch out a bit before you continue so that it's very loose on the needle. If you let your stitches snug up, you'll be screwed. You'll have to tug like the dickens, stretching out the leather to jam your needle in. Best to pay attention and keep it slack.

It might be easier to knit through the back loop sometimes, especially on the center stitches.

INSTRUCTIONS

CO 2 sts.

Work 1'/30cm of 2-st I-cord.

CO 3 more sts—5 sts.

Work 1'/30cm of 5-st I-cord.

K2tog, k3.

Work 1'/30cm 4-st I-cord.

K2tog, k2.

Work 1'/30cm 3-st I-cord.

K2tog, k1.

Work 1'/30cm 2-st I-cord.

K2tog.

Switch to crochet hook, chain until you're out of leather, and fasten off.

Loop beginning 2-st I-cord back on itself. Fasten down through top of 5-st I-cord with a zip tie and snip off the end.

Slip the rubber tubing over the tip of the whip, draw it back toward the loop side, and snug it into place. It should be snug, but if you knit tight and it's loose at all, slip it down and fasten on a couple more zip ties around the top, or wrap extra leather or rubber bands, and then work it back into place.

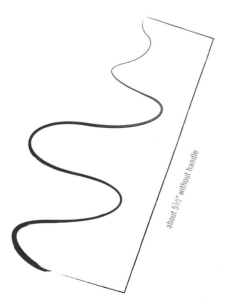

about 5½" without handle

Dress-Up

WHEN I WORKED in an office, I was forever trying to convince my coworkers that we should adopt uniforms. Tyvek hazmat suits at the investment bank or big furry animal costumes at the soulless dot-com. My coworkers brushed me off, and whenever I recommended it to management, they just laughed nervously. "If I were the boss," I'd grumble, "you'd be in a bear suit."

I love uniforms. I love uniforms and their close cousin, costumes. My love of uniforms goes back to my awkward transition from Catholic to public school. At All Saints, I knew what I was wearing. Every day. Thanks to the crisp and sturdy man-made fabrics of school uniforms (and the prepubescent no-stink factor), I could even wear my uniform to bed and sleep in a little later, but still look perfectly normal the following day. When I moved to Texas and enrolled in public grade school, this simply was not the case. When I overslept and scrambled to grab the closest thing, I found myself running to the bus, too late to turn back, in two left shoes or the T-shirt I'd worn the day before.

Accustomed to a school uniform and homemade dress and play clothes, I had no clothes consciousness. So initially, I let my mother dress me. In retrospect, I realize my mom must share my penchant for costumes, because on my first day of public school, she dressed me in what can only be described as a cowboy outfit: plaid Western shirt, Rustler jeans, and cheap tan cowboy boots along with a matching belt and large buckle, all purchased at the Don's Western Wear we had visited on our drive to our new home. (There was also a cheap straw cowboy hat, which intuition bade me leave at home.) I'm still not sure whether she honestly believed the kids dressed that way in suburban Houston (all evidence in our oil-money country club neighborhood pointed to the contrary), or whether she was a terrible sadist. On picture day, she put me in a homemade blue velvet dress I had outgrown over the summer, white knee socks, and black patent Mary Janes, with my hair up in a bun on top of my head. Everyone else dressed like a normal kid, in jeans and T-shirts and tennis shoes. I only had one friend that year, a transplant from California whose mother swore a lot and whose young siblings had tiny, excess fingers and toes.

Eventually, I recognized that my best hope for avoiding serious fashion blunders was to adopt costumelike outfits as much as possible. If I try to dress up as something, I always look better. Whether this means I'm something that passes (Glamour Girl, Fallen Angel, Uptight Schoolmarm, Career Gal) or something sillier (Naughty Nurse, Bunny) depends on my mood, the season, and my tolerance of oglers. Dressing up always soothes me somehow. I can climb outside of doubts and boredom and pretend to be who I really am. Besides, when you're in costume, you always feel mischievous. It's a good way to feel.

... Dressing up always soothes me somehow. I can climb outside of doubts and boredom and pretend to be who I really am.

Nursie

Sadly, the wonderful nurse uniforms of yesteryear have gone the way of the dodo, and you're unlikely to see a modern nurse in anything but dumpy scrubs. Luckily, the Naughty Nurse has become a fantasy standard, so nurse whites will live forever, if only in television, porn, and novelty sex costume catalogs. If you want something a bit nicer for your nursecepades, here's a dandy little felted nurse cap. It knits up quickly in a superbulky brushed alpaca that felts like a dream. After several unfortunate failed intarsia versions, I decided to go with needle felting. It prevents fiber bleed and bunching from the extra bulk of all those intarsia tails. Plus, it's fun! Alternatively, you can embroider your cross and trim, after felting, using a diagonal satin stitch with a slip stitch outline for the cross and a slip stitch or chain stitch for the trim.

SIZING
One size

YARN
2 balls Karabella *Brushed Alpaca* (50g; 35yd/32m; 100% alpaca), 0077 off white (A)

1 ball (or a few yards leftovers) Knit Picks *Decadence* (100g; 121yd/111m; 100% superfine alpaca), 23758 winter berry* (B)

You could substitute other red scrap wool, but the color and sheen are exactly perfect, and the rest of the ball would make a luxurious scarf.

NEEDLES & NOTIONS
US 13/9mm needles, or for gauge

Large, sharp embroidery needle

Wooden clothespins

Cotton pads

FOR NEEDLE FELTING ONLY (SHOWN WITH NEEDLE FELTING)
Felting needle(s)

Large chunk of Styrofoam or foam rubber

GAUGE
ALWAYS CHECK YOUR GAUGE! Measure unwashed and unblocked, just relaxed and patted flat (NOT smoothed out)

Stockinette st, A: 8 sts = 4"/10cm

INSTRUCTIONS

When complete, the hat is folded in such a way that both sides are the RS (or the WS, depending on your perspective). For the purpose of knitting the cap, the RS is the side that *starts* as the knit side (the vertical cuff, where the little red cross would go). To compound the problem, the stockinette stitch starts with a purl row for a crisper edge, so you might get your odd and even rows mixed up as well. To make things easy, mark the correct RS (initial knit row for stockinette stitch) by pinning a scrap of yarn to it before you start flipping the direction of the pattern.

Spit splice the ends of the 2 balls rather than knotting. The splice will disappear entirely in the felting, and you'll avoid a bulky lump.

You'll knit this in stockinette st, slipping the first of every row and knitting the last for a smooth edge. Don't worry about curl; that will be corrected in felting and blocking.

CAP FRONT

CO 11 sts, PM, CO 15 sts, PM, CO 11 sts—36 sts.

Starting with a (WS) P row, knit 11 rows in stockinette st, slipping first st and knitting last st all rows.

FOLD LINE

Now you'll work everything from the curve down in reverse stockinette st, so that when you fold the cap, all the public sides are stockinette st.

Row 12 (RS): Sl 1, k10, k2, p11, k2, k11.

Row 13 (WS): Sl 1, p10, k15, p10, k1.

Row 14: Sl 1, k9, p1, p15, p1, k10.

Row 15: Sl 1, p7, k3, k15, k3, p7, k1.

Row 16: Sl 1, k6, p4, p15, p4, k7 (your first ball should end here).

Row 17: Sl 1, p4, k6, k15, k6, p4, k1.

Row 18: Sl 1, k3, p7, p15, p7, k4.

Row 19: Sl 1, p2, k8, k15, k8, p2, k1.

Row 20: Sl 1, k1, p9, p15, p9, k2.

Row 21: Sl 1, k to end.

Row 22: Sl 1, p to 1 st from end, k1.

SIDE FLAP

Now you'll begin shaping the tabs that will fold into the crown of the cap. You'll work the first flap, BO, rejoin yarn to work the next flap, and so on.

Row 1 (WS): Sl 1, k6, k2tog, k2—10 sts. Turn.

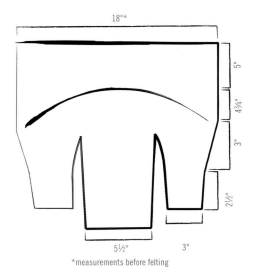

18"*

5"

4¾"

3"

2½"

5½"   3"

*measurements before felting

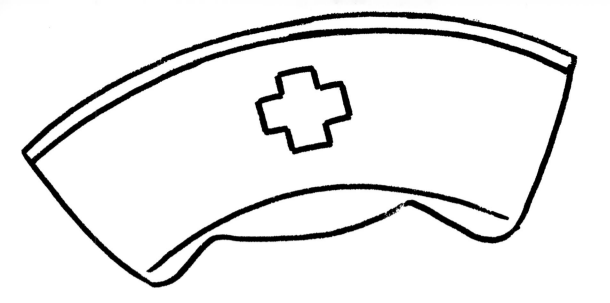

Row 2 (RS): Sl 1, p1, p2tog, p5, k1—9 sts. Turn.

Row 3: Sl 1, k4, k2tog, k2—8 sts. Turn.

Row 4: Sl 1, p1, p2tog, p3, k1—7 sts. Turn.

Row 5: Sl 1, k6. Turn.

Row 6: Sl 1, p5, k1. Turn.

Row 7: Sl 1, k2, k2tog, k2—6 sts. Turn.

Work 5 rows in reverse stockinette st (RS = purls), always slipping the 1st st and knitting last.

BO knitwise.

CENTER FLAP

With WS facing you, rejoin yarn at right side of center section.

Rows 1 (WS)–4 (RS): Work just those 15 center sts back and forth in reverse stockinette st (RS = purls), slipping every 1st st and knitting every last.

Row 5: Sl 1, k1, k2tog, k7, ssk, k2—13 sts.

Rows 6–14: Continue in reverse stockinette st, slipping every first st and knitting every last.

Row 15: Sl 1, p1, p2tog, p5, ptog tbl, p1, K1—11 sts.

Rows 16–19: Reverse stockinette st.

BO knitwise.

SIDE FLAP

With WS facing you, rejoin yarn at right of remaining flap.

Row 1 (WS): Sl 1, k1, k2tog, k7—10 sts. Turn.

Row 2 (RS): Sl 1, p5, p2tog, p1, k1—9 sts. Turn.

Row 3: Sl 1, k1, k2tog, k5—8 sts. Turn.

Row 4: Sl 1, p3, p2tog, p1, k1—7 sts. Turn.

Row 5: Sl 1, k6. Turn.

Row 6: Sl 1, p5, k1. Turn.

Row 7: Sl 1, k1, k2tog, k3–6 sts. Turn.

Work 5 rows in reverse stockinette st (RS =purls), always slipping 1st st and knitting last.

BO knitwise. Weave in an 1–2" of each end (long ends will bulk it up more than necessary in felting).

FELTING AND FINISHING

Wearing rubber gloves to protect your hands, felt by hand in hot water with a few drops of dish soap. Don't machine felt, because this is a very sticky yarn and you may well end up with a giant ball of hard felt. Besides, wet and knitted, this fabric has a very unusual texture, almost like melted cheese, and it's great fun to felt.

When the fabric is dense and even, roll out excess water in several towels and fold along curve between stockinette st and reverse stockinette st.

Use cotton-padded clothespins to hold the cap's shape while it dries. It may take a day or longer, during which time you might want to occasionally rearrange the clothespins, just to be on the safe side.

After the fabric completely dries, needle felt or embroider the cross into place, assemble cap, and affix flaps to crown with little French knots or minute Xs made of B, using the large, sharp embroidery needle.

Cap Embellishments

EMBROIDERY

Using B and a large, sharp embroidery needle and in split st or stem st, work a line of red, about ¼"/6mm from edge, along cap cuff.

Trace and cut out cross motif and pin to center of cuff. Outline cross in split st, then remove cutout and fill in cross in satin stitch.

NEEDLE FELTING

Working over a large piece of foam rubber or Styrofoam (finally, a use for all that packaging!), position a strand of B near edge of cuff, about ¼"/6mm down.

Prick with felting needle at ⅛"/3mm intervals to position yarn, then gradually increase speed and frequency of pokes (and number of needles, if you have a holder) until it's well worked in.

Trace and cut out cross motif, then trim about 1/16"/1.5mm off all edges.

Pin cross motif to center of cuff.

Separate a 12"/30.5cm piece of B into 2 strands. Smooth one of the strands with damped fingers to minimize fuzziness, then outline edge of cross as closely as possible, pricking into place with felting needle as you go. When outline is secure, remove cutout and gradually fill in cross with more yarn.

After you've worked it in well, you can manipulate individual stray fibers by changing the direction of your needle.

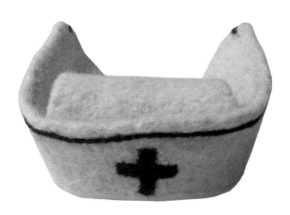

Siren

This restrictive tail is knit with a continuous strand of shiny, stretchy Patons Katrina, worked together with 1–3 additional strands of (mostly novelty) yarn. You'll freeform the strands you hold and drop, creating mock-intarsia blocks of contrasting or coordinating color, and dropping and adding the same color groups over blotches across rows to avoid a stripy look. You don't need to work in yarn ends properly—the Katrina is your constant, keeping the fabric together, and the other strands can be added and released at will. Cut strands when you drop them, or you'll end up with a giant yarn barf tangle, since you're knitting in the round. The yarn ends add to the seaweedy effect.

Women's S (M, L, XL)

Where no parentheses are used, instructions/
quantities apply to all sizes

YARN, ETC.

I've listed the exact yarns used here, but as long as you
carry the *Katrina* throughout, you can use your imagination
(and your stash). Since you'll work with 3 strands throughout, you'll want a total of 1200–2000 yd/1097–1829m
(roughly 400yd/366m total for each ball of *Katrina* your size
uses) of various (mostly textured) yarns in a sea-inspired
palette, in addition to the *Katrina*. I used a blue/green/
purple range, with tiny shots of orange, yellow, brown, and
acid green. I also really like the Patons *Carmen* in steel for
its supersoft texture and smoky underwater appearance, so
I've called for it specifically near the waist.

3 (4, 4, 5) balls Patons *Katrina* (100g; 163yd/150m;
92% rayon, 8% polyester), 10712 limon (A)

Plus an assortment of sea-hued novelty yarns

Tail shown uses:

3 balls Patons *Carmen* (50g; 64yd/58m; 36%
polyester, 64% nylon), 07108 steel (B)

1 ball Patons *Pebbles* (50g; 54yd/49m; 45%
polyester, 46% acrylic, 9% wool), 10110 blue
marble (C)

1 ball Bernat *Matrix* (50g; 140yd/128m; 38%
polyester, 62% nylon), 02712 acid axis (D)

1 ball Bernat *Eyelash* (50g; 77yd/70m; 100%
nylon), 35005 wild (E)

1 ball Lion Brand *Fancy Fur* (50g; 39yd/35m;
55% polyamide, 45% polyester), 254 stained
glass (F)

1 ball Lion Brand *Fancy Fur* (50g; 39yd/35m;
55% polyamide, 45% polyester), 257 stormy
sea (G)

1 ball Lion Brand *Lion Boucle* (70g; 57yd/52m;
79% acrylic, 20% mohair, 1% nylon), 202
lime blue (H)

2 skeins Lion Brand *Color Waves* (85g;
125yd/113m; 83% acrylic, 17% polyester),
350 night sky (I)

1 skein Lion Brand *Color Waves* (85g;
125yd/113m; 83% acrylic, 17% polyester),
347 purple vista (K)

2 balls Lion Brand *Moonlight Mohair* (50g;
82yd/75m; 57% acrylic, 28% mohair, 9%
cotton, 6% metallic polyester), 205 glacier
bay (L)

1 ball Lion Brand *Moonlight Mohair* (50g;
82yd/75m; 57% acrylic, 28% mohair, 9%
cotton, 6% metallic polyester), 206 purple
mountains (M)

1 hank Berroco *Optik* (50g; 87yd/80m; 48%
cotton, 21% acrylic, 20% mohair, 8% metallic, 3% polyester), 4944 cadaquez (N)

1 hank Berroco *Hush* (50g; 52yd/48m; 100%
nylon), 6310 rockabye blue (O)

1 ball Berroco *Lavish* (50g; 55yd/50m; 40%
nylon, 32% wool, 15% polyester, 13%
acrylic), 7334 cadaquez (P)

1 hank Blue Sky Alpacas *Dyed Cotton* (100g;
150yd/137m; 100% organically grown cotton), 605 cumin (Q)

1 ball Knit One Crochet Too (K1C2) *Jam* (50g;
93yds/85m; 100% nylon), 835 golden pear

2 yd/1.8m elastic, ¼"/6cm wide (R)

NEEDLES AND NOTIONS
US 11/8mm 24"/61cm circular needles, or for
gauge

US 7/4.5mm) 16"/40.5cm) circular needles, or
for gauge

K crochet hook

3 colors of stitch markers (1 for first color, 20–30 for
2nd color, 10–15 for 3rd color)

Locking stitch markers

Stitch holder

GAUGE
Will vary with yarns used

INSTRUCTIONS

This garment is more about restricting movement and looking yummy than serious binding, so the fit is soft and comfortable, with denser ribbing around the waist and ankles to hold it nicely in place. If you prefer a more bound sensation (or just a slinkier line) use US 10 needles (or 2 sizes down from gauge) instead.

If you're making this as a costume instead of as a fetish binder, use larger needles throughout and eliminate the extra 8"/20.5cm of length before the flukes. Seam each fluke only halfway. The stockinette edges will curl under gracefully at the open end. If you're not the topless type, freeform knit a large, irregular piece of "kelp" and tie it around your chest, or knit the Cave Girl top using your leftover yarn, adding and dropping strands just as you did with the tail.

Standing, measure from your hip bone to the ground.

WAIST

The tubular cast on is a bit tedious, especially with novelty yarns, but it creates a gorgeous, smooth, hidden casing for elastic that you'll need to deal with the weight of the tail.

Using cotton waste yarn and K crochet hook, chain 23 (26, 27, 29). With A and B held together, pick up stitches and work tubular cast-on with larger needles as directed in "Techniques" (p.136)—45 (51, 54, 57) sts. Once you're finished, you can unravel the chain, but don't pull out the drawstring.

Join yarn, PM (first color).

Knot the two ends of the waste yarn drawstring together, just to be safe.

Switch to k2, p1 rib, PM after every P st, alternating marker colors every 3rd rib.

When you've finished the row, the start of the row will be one color, the 1st 2 of every 3 ribs will be marked with a 2nd color, and the 3rd of every 3 ribs will be marked with a 3rd color. (There aren't 3 ribs in the last set in every size, so don't worry if you have a few spare ribs.)

After the 1st 1"/2.5cm, keep the *Katrina* in the mix until the tail, but add and drop other strands at random to achieve a highly irregular effect. You can weave in yarn ends or not, as you like. It's all free form and crazy, so have fun! Use 2 strands at all times, and 3 strands most of the time.

Work 2"/5cm k2, p1 rib.

HIP SHAPING

You'll increase to the hips by increasing ribs with an M1 from k2 to k3, working with ⅓ of the ribs at a time. This is where the alternating colored markers come into play, acting as flags.

Increase every 3rd rib by inserting an M1 inc: *K2, p1, k2, p1, k1, M1, k1, p1, repeat from * to end, working any remaining stitches in pattern.

Work 5 rnds in pattern.

Inc second of every 3 ribs: *K2, p1, k1, M1, k1, p1, k3, p1, repeat from * to end, working any remaining sts in pattern.

Work 5 rnds in pattern.

Inc remaining ribs: *K1, M1, k1, p1, k3, p1, k3, p1, repeat from * to end, working any remaining sts in pattern.

Work 10 rnds in pattern (k3, p1 rib).

LEG SHAPING

Now you'll taper back down the opposite way, decreasing ribs from k3 p1 to k2 p1, ⅓ at a time. Then you'll decrease again, ending in a k1, p1 rib.

Decrease first of every 3 ribs: *K1, k2tog, p1, k3, p1, k3, p1, repeat from * to end, working any remaining sts in pattern.

Work 10 rnds in pattern.

Decrease the 2nd of every 3 ribs: *K2, p1, k1, k2tog, p1, k3, p1, repeat from * to end, working any remaining sts in pattern.

Work 10 rnds in pattern.

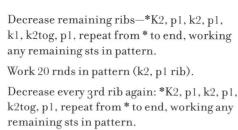

Decrease remaining ribs—*K2, p1, k2, p1, k1, k2tog, p1, repeat from * to end, working any remaining sts in pattern.

Work 20 rnds in pattern (k2, p1 rib).

Decrease every 3rd rib again: *K2, p1, k2, p1, k2tog, p1, repeat from * to end, working any remaining sts in pattern.

Work 10 rnds in pattern.

Decrease the second rib of every set again: *K2, p1, k2tog, p1, k1, p1, repeat from * to end, working any remaining stitches in pattern.

Work 10 rnds in pattern

Decrease remaining ribs: *K2tog, p1, k1, p1, k1, p1, repeat from * to end, working any remaining stitches in pattern.

ANKLE SHAPING

Switch to smaller needles. Continue k1, p1 rib, dropping all markers except 1st marker at beg of rnd.

Continue in pattern until tail measures your hip-to-floor measurement + 8"/20.5cm. Using locking stitch makers, PM after 15 (17, 18, 19) sts, finish rnd, and replace row marker with locking marker.

FLUKES

Switch back to larger needles.

Inc every rib: *K1, M1, p1, repeat from * to end—45 (51, 54, 57) sst.

Work 1 rnd in pattern, k2, p1 rib.

Inc every rib: *K1, M1, k1, p1, repeat from * to end—60 (68, 72, 76) sts.

Work 3 rnds in pattern, k3, p1 rib.

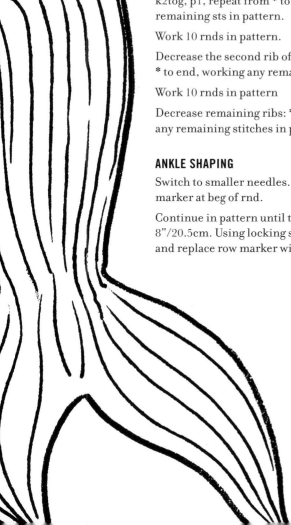

SPLIT TAIL

The flukes will be divided at the markers (center front and back). If there's a particular patch you really like or dislike, you can rearrange the markers to remark centers, so the tail is shown to its best advantage. If you move the markers, keep them 30 (34, 36, 38) sts apart and with the 1st marker at the beginning of a rib; knit in pattern up to the 1st repositioned marker.

Transfer last half of sts (from 2nd marker, on) to st holder.

FLUKE 1

For all sizes except L:
Using the remaining half of the stitches on your larger needles, work row in pattern to 1 st from end, M1, p 1—31 (35, 0, 39) sts. Turn work.

K 1, M1, continue in pattern to end of row—32 (36, 0, 40) sts.

All sizes:

Work 10 (10, 12, 10) rows in pattern, ending with WS row.

TAPER FLUKE

Using locking st markers, PM on the needle after the 8th st from either end.

Work in pattern to marker, *K1, k2tog, p1, repeat from * to marker, work in pattern to end.

Work 5 rows in pattern, ending with a WS row.

Work in pattern to marker, *K2tog, p1, repeat from * to marker, work in pattern to end.

K5 rows in pattern, ending with a WS row.

*K1 k2tog p1, repeat from * to marker, *k2tog, p2tog, repeat from * to marker, *k1 k2tog, p1, repeat from * to end.

Work WS row.

* K2tog, p1, repeat from * to marker, *k1, p1, repeat from * to marker, *k1, k2tog, p1, repeat from * to end.

Work WS row pattern.

All RS rows, work until only 2 sts between markers: K1, p1, k1, p1, *k2tog, p2tog, repeat from * to marker, k1, p1, k1, p1. (WS rows continue in pattern.)

*K2tog, repeat from * to end. Repeat every RS row (WS rows purled) until 1 st remains, then BO.

FLUKE 2

Transfer sts back to larger needles. Work exactly as for Fluke 1, except:

Work 16 (16, 18, 16) rows before tapering instead of 10 (10, 12, 10).

FINISHING

Seam flukes.

Siren Variations

If the idea of freeforming scares you, or you just prefer more uniform textures and colors, stick with 3 yarns: *Katrina,* plus 8 (10, 10, 13) balls Patons *Carmen* (50g; 64yd/58m; 36% polyester, 64% nylon) in 07108 steel for airy, fuzzy softness and dimension, and 6 (7, 8, 9) balls of multi-colored, multi-textured Berroco *Optik* (50g; 87yd/80m, 48% cotton, 21% acrylic, 20% mohair, 8% metallic, 3% polyester) in 4844 cadaquez for built-in variation.

If you get bored, add a little adventure by breaking and rejoining yarn periodically to create thinner patches or knitting in 1–3' lengths of random waste yarn from your scrap bag or mystery stash. You can also shave portions afterward with electric clippers to break up wide bands of color or to create worn or bare areas, or add random fringe anywhere along the tail or flukes.

For a more stylized, sophisticated tail, or for a dreamy skirt (work as usual through the hip increases, then knit in pattern to your chosen length), use 4 (5, 6, 7) hanks of Noro *Big Kureyon* (100g; 175yd/160m; 100% wool), color 12, on US 11 needles (still changing to US 7 at the base if you're making the tail).

Fish Net

Our siren's net doubles as the extralong, lush, airy scarf, shown at right.

Spread out, it's a lovely coverlet over a white or solid color comforter. Jen, who knit the net, made it a mate and hung the pair as lacy curtains. Or use it as a room divider in a child's sea-themed bedroom: spread and secure to rods at top and bottom, then suspend from the ceiling; use clothespins or paperclips to catch pictures and other small treasures.

YARN
10 balls Berroco *Optik* (50g; 87yd/80m; 48% cotton, 21% acrylic, 20% mohair, 8% metallic, 3% polyester), 4944 cadaquez

NEEDLES & NOTIONS
US 35/19mm needles (gauge not critical)

INSTRUCTIONS

CO 86 sts.

Row 1: K1 *k2tog, yo, repeat from * until last st, k1.

Row 2 (and all even rows): Purl

Row 3: K2, *k2tog, yo, repeat from * until last 2 sts, k2.

Repeat until 86"/218.5cm spread flat (or finish off ball of yarn), ending with a purl row.

BO. Weave in ends.

Arrgh!

SIZING
Unisex M (L)
Where no parentheses are used, instructions/quantities apply to all sizes

YARN
1 hank (or about 20m leftovers) Blue Sky Alpacas *Sport Weight 100% Alpaca* (50g; 110yds/100m; 100% alpaca), 100 black

NEEDLES & NOTIONS
US 5/3.75mm double-pointed needles, or size necessary to achieve gauge
US 6/4mm needle
point protectors (so you can use your dpns to knit both patch and I-cord)
Dish soap
Towel

GAUGE
ALWAYS CHECK YOUR GAUGE! Measure unwashed and unblocked, just relaxed and patted flat (NOT smoothed out)
Garter st, 2 strands A: 17 sts = 4"/10cm

Everyone loves pirates. They're dirty, rowdy, mean, crude, scary. They live by their own questionable code— like bikers, before everyone's dad bought a Harley. They're what you would be if you could finally abandon both manners and soap. But if you're not quite there yet, you can always capture that renegade spirit (and poor depth perception) by donning an eye patch. This one knits in a jiffy and shrinks to a nice dense, curlicue alpaca felt. If you prefer a smooth version, substitute plain wool. Arrgh!

This whole project only uses about 20m of yarn, so it's brilliant for yarn ends.

INSTRUCTIONS

Using 2 strands, CO 8 (10) sts.

Rows 1–5: Sl 1, k to end.

Row 6: Sl 1, k2tog, k to end.

Thereafter, decrease every 4th row until you have 5 (6) sts.

FORM DART

Without turning work, pick up and knit through each of the chain sts along the straight edge. At first, this is going to leave you with a pretty tight, awkward row on your needle. But as you knit away from the turn, it will get easier to knit.

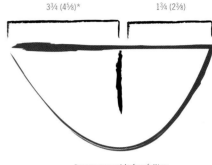

*measurement before felting

Nurse Elle Variation

From the *Kill Bill Vol. 1* hospital scene.

Knit patch as directed, substituting 000 natural white for the black Blue Sky Alpacas *Sport Weight 100%* Alpaca (50g; 110yds/100m; 100% alpaca). When it's completely dry, use a few yards leftover Knit Picks *Decadence* (100g; 121yd; 100% superfine alpaca, 23758 winterberry) to embroider or needle-felt the red cross (see Nursie embellishment instructions on p. 112 and scale down cross to fit).

TAPER SIDE AND EDGE

Continue decreasing at the beginning of every 4th row 2 (3) more times. Then, decrease every other row until you're out of stitches.

Using US 6 needle, pick up and knit and immediately, *loosely*, BO each st along the top edge (alternately, you can crochet the edge), leaving last live st on your needle. Keep the BO loose so this doesn't pull everything too snug when you felt it.

STRAP

Measure around your head where you'll want the patch to go. The cord will shrink in felting, so don't deduct much for the patch; take the full measurement for medium, and subtract 1"/2.5cm for the large. Mine was 22", but I have a small head.

Remove point protectors and pick up and knit 2 more sts at corner edge.

Knit I-cord to length. BO and sew onto opposite corner of the patch.

FINISHING

Felt in the washing machine or by hand. The alpaca felt is ready when it's all curlicued like Karakul fur. Smooth the cord and try the patch on. Stretch cord a bit if necessary to fit, but don't overdo it—you want it snug.

Tugging gently at the sides to reshape, pull the edges of the patch to match picture. Patch should be lopsided, an oval that is somewhat flattened on top and tapers in towards the nose on the bottom edge. Which side you stretch/taper will depend on the side you intend to wear it on (and you can always pop it inside out later).

Once you have the overall shape right, push outward a bit to keep it slightly bulged (not flat). Air dry completely before wearing, matey.

Into the Woods

This sexy little cape makes excellent wolf bait. Knitted in a superbulky wool-alpaca blend and felted into dense, thick fabric, this cape is heavy enough for fall outerwear, sassy enough for indoor play.

For serious winter outerwear, add several balls (you'll get about 6 extra rows per ball) and continue in stockinette stitch before shaping hem and finishing.

Use a row of heavy hooks and eyes or frog closures down the front, and, if you like, cut in slash pockets and trim them with wide velvet ribbon in a matching or contrast color.

SIZING
Women's S/M (L/XL)

Where no parentheses are used, instructions/quantities apply to all sizes

YARN, ETC.
14 (16) balls Blue Sky Alpacas *Bulky Hand Dyes* (100g; 45yd/41m; 50% alpaca, 50% wool), 1010 red

5 yd/4.5m bulky waste yarn (cotton is easiest)

Embroidery floss or button thread to match yarn

Heavy-duty hook and eye, or closure of choice

NEEDLES AND NOTIONS
US 15/10mm circular needles (30"/76cm or longer), or for gauge

Sharp embroidery needle and thread

Detergent

Towels

Plastic grocery bags, dry cleaning bags, or garbage bags (or stuff plastic w/ crumpled newspaper)

Large cork board (for blocking; optional but handy)

FOR MACHINE FELTING ONLY
Large zippered dog bed cover, crib duvet cover, etc.

FOR HAND FELTING ONLY
Rubber gloves

PRE-FELTING GAUGE
ALWAYS CHECK YOUR GAUGE! Measure unwashed and unblocked, just relaxed and patted flat (NOT smoothed out).

Stockinette st: 8 sts = 4"/10cm

INSTRUCTIONS

All M1 increases are invisible increases. All short rows should have a short row wrap before the turn. Knit/purl all wraps in as you pass them. (See "Techniques," p. 134 for help.)

HOOD

CO 30 (38) sts with waste yarn.

Knit 1 row.

Switch to main yarn, k7 rows stockinette st.

Row 8 (RS): K10 (12), M1, k3 (5), M1, k4, M1, k3 (5), M1, k10 (12)—34 (42) sts.

Rows 9–15: Stockinette st.

Row 16: K11 (13), M1, k4 (6), M1, k4, M1, k4 (6), M1, k11 (13) —38 (46) sts.

Rows 17–23: Stockinette st.

Row 24: K12 (14), M1, k5 (7), M1, k4, M1, k5 (7), M1, k12 (14) —42 (50) sts.

Rows 25–29: Stockinette st.

HOOD SHAPING

K18 (22), wrap and turn.

P14, wrap and turn.

K34, wrap and turn (knitting in one wrap along the way).

P14, wrap and turn.

K to end (knitting in one wrap along the way).

P row (purling in two wraps along the way).

Repeat last 6 rows.

Work 5 (9) rows stockinette st.

Transfer ½ of sts to a 2nd needle and seam with kitchener st.

COLLAR

Remove waste yarn and carefully transfer live stitches to circular needles.

Holding fabric with knit side facing you, ktbl across entire row—30 (38) sts.

NAPE

You'll shape the nape with short rows, using a short row wrap before turning each row.

P23 (27), wrap and turn.

K16, wrap and turn.

P to end (purling in one wrap along the way).

K across (knitting on one wrap along the way).

P1 row.

SHOULDERS

The shoulders have increases at several places. It can get really complicated, so after every change, there's a little cheat sheet of what your completed row should look like, making it a snap to work back and correct your error before you really get off course. The double lines indicate your contrasting-color shoulder markers.

K2 (3), PM (#1A), k3 (4), PM (#2A), k2 (3), PM (#3A—shoulder—contrast color), k2 (3), PM (#4A), k4 (5), PM (#5A), k4 (5), PM (#5B), k4, PM (#4B), k2 (3), PM (#3B—shoulder—contrast color), k2 (3), PM (#2B), k3 (4), PM (#1B), k2 (3).

Purl 1 row.

S/M: 2 | 3 | 2 || 2 | 4 | 4 | 4 | 2 || 2 | 3 | 2

L/XL: 3 | 3 | 3 || 3 | 5 | 4 | 5 | 3 || 3 | 3 | 3

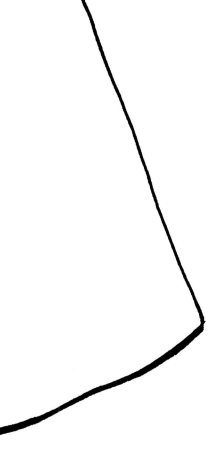

Now you'll M1 increase 1 st before and 1 st after each marker. Because the 1st row of the smaller size has several clumps of 2 sts, we'll divide our 1st increase between 2 rows.

FOR SIZES S/M:
K1, M1, k1, k1, M1, k1, M1, k1, k1, M1, k1, k1, M1, k1, k1, M1, k2, M1, k1, k1, M1, k2, M1, k1, k1, M1, k2, M1, k1, k1, M1, k1, k1, M1, k1, k1, M1, k1, M1, k1, k1, M1, k1—46 sts.

Purl row.

K3, k5, k2, M1, k1, k1, M1, k2, k6, k6, k6, k2, M1, k1, k1, M1, k2, k5, k3—50 sts.

S/M Result: 3 | 5 | 4 || 4 | 6 | 6 | 6 | 4 || 4 | 5 | 3

FOR SIZES L/XL:
M1 1 st before and 1 st after each marker—58 sts.

Purl.

Knit.

L/XL Result: 4 | 5 | 5 || 5 | 7 | 6 | 7 | 5 || 5 | 5 | 4

BOTH SIZES:
Work 3 (5) rows in stockinette st.

Knit row, placing M1 inc 1 st before and after every marker—66 (78) sts.

S/M: 4 | 7 | 6 || 6 | 8 | 8 | 8 | 6 || 6 | 7 | 4

L/XL: 5 | 7 | 7 || 7 | 9 | 8 | 9 | 7 || 7 | 7 | 5

Work 5 (7) rows in stockinette st.

Knit, placing M1 inc 1 st before and 1 st after every marker—90 (98) sts

S/M: 5 | 9 | 8 || 8 | 10 | 10 | 10 | 8 || 8 | 9 | 5

L/XL: 6 | 9 | 9 || 9 | 11 | 10 | 11 | 9 || 9 | 9 | 6

Work 7 rows stockinette st.

Knit, placing M1 inc 1 st before and 1 st after every marker—110 (118) sts.

S/M: 6 | 11 | 10 || 10 | 12 | 12 | 12 | 10 || 10 | 11 | 6

L/XL: 7 | 11 | 11 || 11 | 13 | 12 | 13 | 11 || 11 | 11 | 7

Now you've finished your shoulder increases. Drop the 3rd marker (the contrasting color) from each side as you purl the next row. The stitches don't change, but the distribution between the markers will. This will affect your future increases, so get it right.

S/M: 6 | 11 | 20 | 12 | 12 | 12 | 20 | 11 | 6

L/XL: 7 | 11 | 22 | 13 | 12 | 13 | 22 | 11 | 7

Work 10 (12) rows stockinette st.

Knit, placing M1 inc one stitch before and after every marker—126 (134) sts.

S/M: 8 | 13 | 22 | 14 | 14 | 14 | 22 | 13 | 8

L/XL: 9 | 13 | 24 | 15 | 14 | 15 | 24 | 13 | 9

HEMLINE SHAPING

Continue in stockinette stitch until you're down to your last ball of yarn. Then you'll make short rows to fill out the hemline.

K112 (116), wrap and turn.

P98, wrap and turn.

K86, wrap and turn.

P74, wrap and turn.

K62, wrap and turn.

P50, wrap and turn.

K to end (knitting in 3 wraps).

P row (knitting in 3 wraps).

1 row seed st.

BO in seed st.

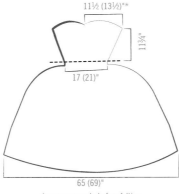

11½ (13½)"*

11¾"

17 (21)"

65 (69)"

* measurements before felting

EDGING

Pick up and knit 3 sts for every 4 rows around perimeter of cape. BO in seed st (K 1, p 1). Weave in about 1" of any yarn ends; trim excess.

You should wet splice this yarn and knit continuously instead of adding new yarn at the end of rows. The yardage of superbulky yarn is relatively low and the body of the cape is relatively wide, so joining only at the side would inflate yarn requirements. Also, because this is a very bulky garment (and it gets denser with felting), splicing yarn means you'll have fewer ends to weave in, keeping the garment streamlined and tidy. And since you're felting it anyway, there's no risk of the splice showing or the ends unraveling.

Wet splicing (AKA spit splicing) is super easy. Gently loosen the fibers at both ends, and then place them, slightly overlapping, in your palm and wet with a little water or spit. Roll firmly between your palms, as you would roll clay into a rope. The moisture and friction felt the pieces together. Even when you're not felting, it's a great way to join 100% animal fibers, with virtually invisible results if done carefully—particularly with soft-twist single-ply yarns like this stuff, Lopi, and other bulky singles.

FELTING

You can hand felt or machine felt the cape. Machine felting will give you a tighter, more matted fabric, which means less stretch over time, a nice feature for a cape. It will also be far less work. Hand felting gives you more control and a fluffier, fuzzy-wuzzier appearance and richer color, but you may not get as dense a fabric, and it might be trying with a garment this large. You'll need a bathtub with a few inches of very hot water, or a washing machine.

Using hot water and a few tablespoons of dish soap, soak cape 20 minutes (either in the bathtub, or in the washing machine tub).

HAND FELTING

Wear rubber gloves and knead the cape like a giant ball of bread dough until you have a dense, tight, hairy knit. Alternately, you can march and twist around on it with your feet. You might need to empty and refill the tub (a strainer on your drain will help prevent clogs—a garment this large sheds lots of fiber). When fabric has fulled evenly, roll out in towels and block.

MACHINE FELTING

Enclose cape in a dog bed cover, small duvet cover, or any very large zippered case. This process will shed a great deal of fiber, especially with mechanical agitation, and you don't want to fuck up your washing machine, even for a stylish cape. (A zippered pillow case will be far too small and you'll end up with a horrid creased and wadded mess.) Using hottest water, a medium cycle, and a few pairs of jeans to keep things rolling, start the wash cycle of your machine. Check on the cape after 10 minutes, then every five minutes until it's rather matted and it has lost stitch clarity. In my front-loading washer, it took about 40 minutes; a top loader will work faster. Spin no longer than 30 seconds, then roll on towels to remove excess water.

BLOCKING

If you've hand felted your cape, your blocking will be fairly laid back. If you've machine felted, you may need to put a little more ass into it, as the fabric will be far less giving.

Try it on and tug lightly (or firmly, as needed) forward on the edges to shape all around the hood, while resisting with your head. Take cape

off, tug firmly all the way around the edges (front and bottom) to get them smooth and even, then pin down so that front edges lie flush together, nice and straight, and hem lies flush as well.

Do not press on sides of cape when you lay it flat—you want the sides to dry without creasing.

Similarly, let the shoulders stay relaxed as the cap dries—you can stuff some wadded plastic grocery bags into the shoulders and sides to keep fabric smooth and allow more air to circulate.

To maintain the nice shape of the head, use a plastic grocery bag stuffed with newspaper balls or shreds.

Let dry completely (which may take a few days).

Finish by sewing a heavy-duty hook and eye, or your closure of choice, at neck with matching embroidery floss. If desired, you can add more closures along the front.

Fast Track
Techniques Demystified

Here are three gorgeous semi-advanced knitting techniques that beginning knitters normally avoid like the plague. Learning them will catapult you out of the Scarf Club and get you thinking creatively and producing advanced and custom garments, lickety-split. There are a bazillion knitting references out there for the basics, but I felt these three deserved special attention. I love them. You will, too. (If you balk at "wasting" time swatching new techniques, see naughtyneedlesknitting.com for a handbag project that will let you practice all 3 techniques and get a project out of it. Hurrah!)

Kitchener Stitch

Kitchener is my very favorite seam. It's so smooth and elegant and invisible, completely disappearing into stockinette. It's magic. And it's also totally easy, once you learn it. It's all based on the rhythm. You can chant this as you go: "[front stitches:] knitwise, slip it off; purlwise, leave it on; [back stitches] purlwise, slip it off; knitwise, leave it on." The only part that's different is the setup and the ending, where you'll only use half of the mantra.

Kitchener is easier when you understand the fundamentals of it. The big mistake beginners make is just threading the yarn through each live stitch once, the way you would, say, closing up the top of a hat worked in the round. That will close the seam, but it will look horrible, and won't be secure or strong. Instead, you'll work the yarn through each and every stitch twice, from opposite directions (but only once at a time), thereby mimicking the little Vs that form in stockinette. You'll work stitches in sets of 4, two each from front and back needle. Each time, you'll work only one half of each of the four stitches. When you work the next set of four, you'll be completing one pair (the stitches you slip off) and working the first half of the next pair (the stitches you leave on). That's why the setup stitch is the second half of your mantra ("purlwise, leave it on" for your first front stitch and "knitwise, leave it on" for your first back stitch): you need to set up the rhythm by working only the first half of each of those first two stitches.

If that was as clear as mud, hang on a second. Once you start doing it, you'll see just what I mean.

Note: While kitchener st will form a smooth, attractive seam on any pattern, this method will only form an invisible seam on stockinette st, reverse stockinette st, or garter st. This is because it mimics a solid row of knitting.

The pieces you're seaming must have the same number of live stitches. If one needle is off, decrease a stitch somewhere in your last row on one side.

The easiest way to set everything up is to either transfer stitches to dpns or to slip both pieces onto either end of a circular needle, so that wrong sides are facing when the needle points are held together. If you're seaming stockinette st or reverse stockinette st, purled sides face in and knit sides face out. If you're seaming garter st, both sides need to have the last knit rows facing inward, so you'll have a row of purl bumps as the last row facing out on both sides. You'll be forming a "knit" row facing out, between your two needles.

With a strand of yarn about four times the length of the area you're seaming (using the live end off the back needle is often convenient), thread a yarn needle.

Hold both needles together in your left hand. I like to separate them with my index finger, leaving the stitches somewhat loose as I go, then adjusting tension at the end.

First the setup. You'll be working the *second* beats of your mantra. Remember, your mantra is "[front needle:] Knitwise, slip it off; **purlwise, leave it on**; [back needle:] purlwise, slip it off; **knitwise, leave it on.**" So the setup takes the second beat from each needle, the bolded beats.

1. SET-UP

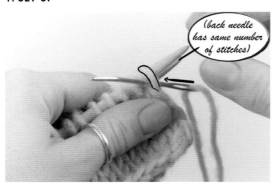

(back needle has same number of stitches)

Purlwise, leave it on. Insert the needle through the first front stitch purlwise. Leaving the stitch on the needle, pull the yarn through.

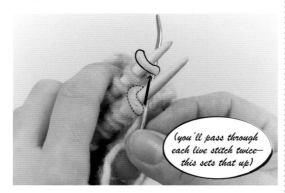

(you'll pass through each live stitch twice—this sets that up)

Knitwise, leave it on. Insert the needle through the first back stitch knitwise. Leaving the stitch on the needle, pull the yarn through. (The dotted line shows the stitch you worked in the previous step.) Now you're ready to get going on the seam, using your little 4-beat mantra.

2. MAIN PATTERN

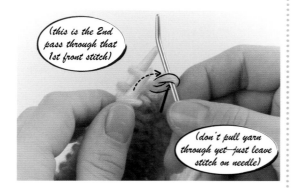

(this is the 2nd pass through that 1st front stitch)

(don't pull yarn through yet—just leave stitch on needle)

Knitwise, slip it off. Insert the yarn needle knitwise through your first front stitch and slip it right off the knitting needle. You're ready to slip this off because this stitch has been passed through twice now: once with the setup, and once with this stitch. No stitch slides off the needle until it's been passed through twice.

(now pull yarn through both stitches)

Purlwise, leave it on. Insert the yarn needle purlwise through your next front stitch. Leaving the stitch on the knitting needle, pull your yarn through, snugging it through both stitches. (The dotted line shows the stitch you slipped off the knitting needle in the previous step.)

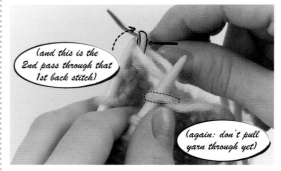

(and this is the 2nd pass through that 1st back stitch)

(again: don't pull yarn through yet)

Purlwise, slip it off. Insert the yarn needle purlwise through your first back stitch and slip it off the knitting needle.

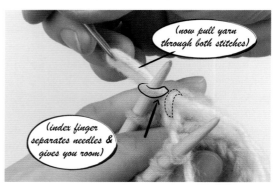

(now pull yarn through both stitches)

(index finger separates needles & gives you room)

Knitwise, leave it on. Insert the yarn needle knitwise through you next back stitch. Leaving the stitch on the knitting needle, pull your yarn through both stitches. (The dotted line shows the stitch you slipped off in the previous step.)

Then you just repeat the process until you're out of stitches. When you're down to the last two stitches (which will each have been passed through once in the previous step), then you'll do the first beats of your mantra. Again, your mantra is "(front needle:) **Knitwise, slip it off**; purlwise, leave it on; (back needle:) **purlwise, slip it off**; knitwise, leave it on." So the finish takes the first beat from each needle, the bolded beats.

3. FINISHING

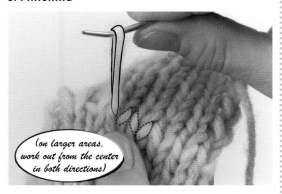

(on larger areas, work out from the center in both directions)

Afterwards, you'll have a single piece of stockinette st with an irregular "knit" row where they've been joined. Now you'll adjust the tension to match the rest of the fabric, making the seam invisible. If you've used the live yarn end off one piece, you'll start at that end and snug up the stitches all the way across. If you've used a separate strand, you can start at the center and work outward. Either way, you may need to make an extra pass or two across to get your tension just right.

(seam is soft, flexible, and completely invisible)

With the tension adjusted, the kitchener st row blends in completely. Voilà!

Photo Note: Current stitches involved are outlined with a solid line. A dotted line outlines stitches used in a previous step. Solid arrows show the direction of your needle. Dotted arrows show motion.

Short Rows

Short rows involve three steps: 1) the rows themselves, turned midway across a normal row and worked back the opposite way; 2) the wrap, which secures the short rows to the rest of the knitting and prevents a hole; and 3) knitting into those wraps so the short rows disappear into the knitting without a trace.

When you first started knitting, you probably inadvertently made a few short rows by setting down your knitting mid-row, then picking it up later and knitting in the wrong direction. You probably discovered your error a few rows later, when you realized that one side of your work was a bit longer than the other, or when you noticed the tell-tale hole that a short row without a short-row wrap creates.

Short rows are just what they sound like: rows that are worked short of the full row before they're turned and worked in the opposite direction. Short rows allow you to sneak some extra real estate into your knitting without disrupting the total stitch count of your pattern. The effect is of a couple of partial rows wedged in gently between complete rows.

You can work short rows just on one side (resulting in a wedge shape, used in Felt Up), or in the center of a piece of knitting, worked in both directions (resulting in a football shape, used in Into the Woods to round the hood, nape, and hemline). Wedges impact the row count on one side (because they're worked all the way to the natural edge), but not the stitch count, while footballs (inserted mid row, then worked short of the edge in both directions) change neither the stitch count nor the row count.

In addition to pattern-specific, prescribed shaping, short rows are a smart and easy way to adjust any pattern when you need a bit more room in one area (bust, bottom, pregnant belly) but don't want to go up a size.

Short row shaping isn't difficult per se, but you should probably practice and get comfortable with it, so you'll be able to spot errors as you make them. Thirty minutes or an hour of practice before you bind off your swatch will pay off in the tears you save unravelling your actual project.

SHORT ROWS & WRAPS

The short row wrap (which is placed at the end of your short row, before your turn your work) prevents a big gaping hole where you've crammed an extra two rows into the middle of all your knitting.

Any time you turn your knitting, you create an edge. That's just as true in the middle of the row as it would be along the proper side. A keyhole scarf is a good example—although you're not working short rows, you *are* turning your work mid-row, and it produces an edge, which disrupts the continuous fabric and results in a hole. (In a keyhole scarf, you'd obviously work several rows' worth of edge, but the initial hole results as soon as you turn your work and knit back the other way.)

When you work short rows, you want to wedge in a few extra rows of knitting *without* disrupting the fabric. So to prevent a mid-row edge, and the subsequent hole it makes, you use a special stitch to anchor your short rows to the rest of your knitting: the short row wrap. It's basically a little lasso that grabs the stitch after the turn and prevents the normal edge that results when you turn work. The little lasso stands out in a row a stockinette st, so you have to knit it in later (see below).

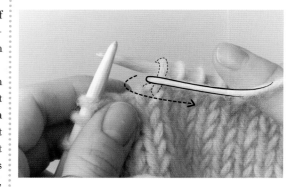

Bring your yarn to the opposite side (front, as shown, if you're knitting; back, if you're purling).

Slip that stitch back onto the left needle, where it started. Your yarn is still where you moved it in the previous step (shown front, as you're knitting).

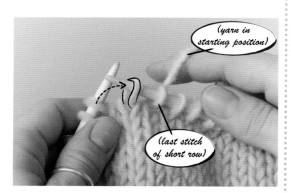

Knit the desired number of short row stitches (pink). Slip the next live stitch purlwise from your left needle to your right needle.

(yarn in starting position)

(last stitch of short row)

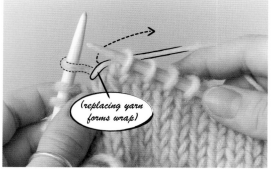

(replacing yarn forms wrap)

Return your yarn to its original position (back if you're knitting; front if you're purling).

Ta da! See that little purl-like bump that forms a noose around the anchor stitch? That's your wrap. Don't worry; we'll work it right into the knitting in the next step, so it will be totally invisible.

KNITTING IN SHORT ROW WRAPS

Now, if you're working in garter st, you can skip the knitting in, because the wrap bumps will blend right into the purl bumps and no one will be the wiser. But if you're working in stockinette stitch, you'll need to work those bumps into your knitting. Otherwise, you'll have an array of what appear to be purls demarking your short row insertions outlines like a little geometry lesson. And you don't want that.

You work the wraps in on the row directly above the wraps, so you only have one chance to catch them (don't even think about fixing them a couple rows up—it's a nightmare). On the knit side, this is all pretty straightforward: you'll knit in the wraps as you hit them. Working across on the purl side, it's harder, because the culprits are on the other side of your work. It's good to hold your work low so you're looking at it from above, making it easier to detect those wraps you need to work in. Just because you're working the wrong side doesn't mean the other side of your work disappears.

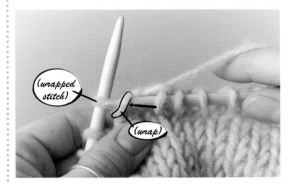

Insert the right needle through the wrap from below, lifting it. (If you're on the wrong/purl side, you'll still be lifting the wrap from below, but it will be on the backside or your stitch instead of in front.)

Still lifting that wrap, insert your needle into the wrapped stitch as usual. Here, we're on the knit side, so we're going knitwise. It's almost as if you were about to k2tog. (If you're on the wrong/purl side, you'll go purlwise, as usual.)

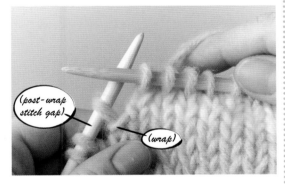

As you approach your wrap, you'll have two clues: the wrap itself (duh, when you're knitting, but easy to miss if you're purling across the wrong side when you hit it), and the gap on your needle that forms right after the wrapped stitch.

Knit them as one stitch. (Purl them as one stitch from the other side.)

Now you're ready to continue knitting (purling) along your row.

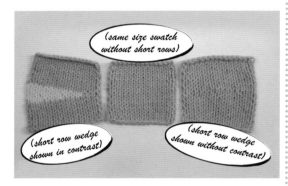

(same size swatch without short rows)

(short row wedge shown in contrast)

(short row wedge shown without contrast)

All 3 swatches have the same stitch and row count, but the two shaped ones have short row wedges (short rows worked in one direction only).

(embedded short rows worked both ways)

The short rows here are worked in both directions.

Tubular Cast-On

I first learned a tubular cast-on in a Nancie Wiseman workshop, and it is brilliant. It's more work than a regular cast-on, but you'll just love it, because it's freaking magic! It's a pretty K1, p1 edge, but more importantly, it creates its own drawstring casing, complete with leader drawstring! So skirts, cuffs, purses, bikinis, halters—anything with a waistband or a drawstring—suddenly become beautifully finished instead of all rigged up and crafty looking. (After learning this, I almost added it to the Cave Girl bikini, but I thought that would be a little too sophisticated for a stone age aesthetic.)

Alternately, you can just pull out the waste yarn instead of using it to draw through elastic or cord or what-have you. Then you've got a very handsome, very stretchy finished ribbed edge that's so much prettier than a regular cast on. It's a lovely sweater cuff or hemline or genius on top-down socks or booties.

The method below, as-is, always produces an odd number of stitches (which is actually better for seaming in most cases), but if you want an even number, there's a variation at the end that will fix you up.

Note: Pick a smooth, non-animal fiber (e.g., cotton, silk, bamboo) for your waste yarn. Wool is too sticky, making removing the provisional stitches less fluid.

1. PROVISIONAL CAST-ON AND SET-UP ROWS

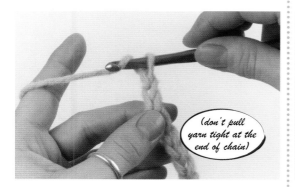

You start by crocheting a chain with waste yarn. Make half as many chains as you need final stitches (round down) +1. Don't pull it too tight when you're finished (that's a habit of mine).

(don't pull yarn tight at the end of chain)

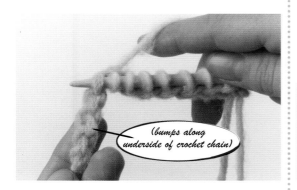

(bumps along underside of crochet chain)

Now you'll flip the chain over so the bumps are facing up. Using your working yarn, you'll pick up one stitch through each bump.

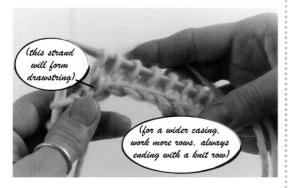

(this strand will form drawstring)

(for a wider casing, work more rows, always ending with a knit row)

Starting with a purl row, work 2 rows in stockinette st. If you're working towards a drawstring/elastic casing, you can work additional rows to accommodate extra width. Just be sure to end with a knit row.

2. FORM CASING (TUBE)

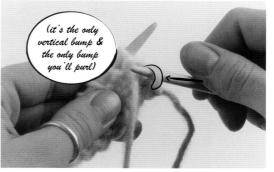

(it's the only vertical bump & the only bump you'll purl)

Turn your work and look at it. There will be one vertical stitch/bump in your working yarn at the beginning of your waste yarn. With your yarn in front, insert your right needle into it purlwise.

(1st live stitch)

Now lift it onto your left needle..

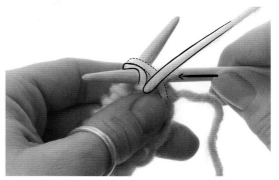

Purl it together with that first stitch that was already there. Now you're ready to get started with the main action.

2. FORM CASING (TUBE) CONTINUED

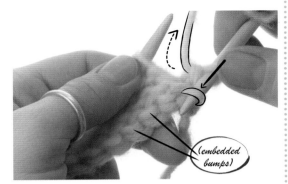

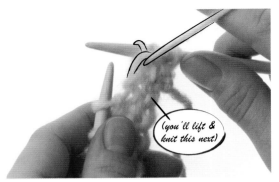

First, move your yarn to the back. Look down at your waste yarn again. See all those little working yarn bumps embedded in your waste yarn? Using your right-hand needle, lift one up. I'm lifting it from the top, but you can lift it from below if that's handier for you.

Work all the way across, knitting the bumps and purling the purls, until you've finished the row. That will give you an odd number of stitches. If you want an even number, work to the last bump to pick up. Leave your yarn in front, pick up the bump and slide it on to the left needle as usual. But instead of knitting it and purling the following stitch, you'll purl them both together. Note: your last 2 stitches will both be purls now.

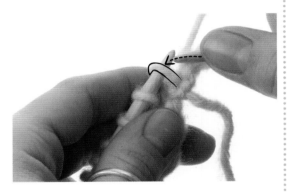

Now slide that bump you just lifted onto your left needle. Knit her.

Here's what you'll have when you finish the casing.

Move your yarn to the front and purl the next live stitch on your left needle.

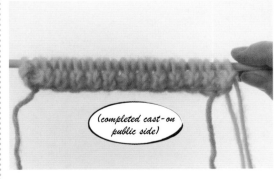

When you turn your work, you'll have a lovely start of K 1, p 1 ribbing. If you're working an even number, be sure to start with a p 1, k 1, which means you'll be purling that first stitch that presents as a knit stitch, to get you back on track after those 2 purl stitches in the previous row.

3. FINISHING

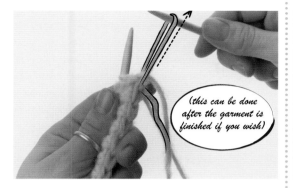

(this can be done after the garment is finished if you wish)

After you've finished your piece, then go back to the end of your crochet chain and unravel it.

(remove waste yarn for a smooth, finished cuff or hemline)

Or pull the waste yarn right out and you have a pretty, stretchy edge.

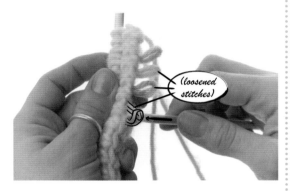

(loosened stitches)

Proceed along the cast-on edge, unraveling every chain loop.

(knot cord or elastic to waste yarn and draw through casing for hidden drawstring or elatic waist, cuff, etc.)

Holding one end of the waste yarn tight, pull firmly on the opposite end to yank out all the loops protruding through your knitting. The result: a drawstring! Magic! Knot your cord or elastic firmly to one end and pull it right through the casing.

Resources

The following resources will help you find all of the yarns and notions called for in this book. See www.naughtyneedlesknitting.com for an assortment of more general knitting resources and any updates to the listings specified here.

Yarn & Tools

LOCAL YARN STORES

The best place to start is somewhere local where you can actually see and touch the fibers. The Daily Knitter has a LYS (local yarn store) directory (also handy when you're traveling): www.dailyknitter.com/shops.html.

YARN COMPANY WEBSITES

If you can't find a specific yarn or a good substitute at your local yarn store, check out the following websites, which offer store locators, email contact, or online retail.

Bernat (www.bernat.com)
Berroco (www.berroco.com)
Blue Sky Alpacas (www.blueskyalpacas.com)
Cascade (www.cascadeyarns.com)
Crystal Palace (www.crystalpalaceyarns.com)
Hello Yarn & Maisy Day Handspun
    (www.helloyarn.com)
Laines du Nord (www.knittingfever.com)
K1C2 (www.knitonecrochettoo.com)
Karabella (www.karabellayarns.com)
Lion Brand (www.lionbrand.com)
Moda Dea (www.modadea.com)
Noro (www.knittingfever.com)
Patons (www.patonsyarn.com)
Reynolds (www.jcacrafts.com)

ONLINE FAVORITES

While online stores may occasionally disappoint (colors or textures can look very different in real life), they're a peach for a great selection and prices. They're also the only place you can get some of the most interesting and gorgeous cottage handspuns and hand-dyed yarns.

Elann (www.elann.com)
Fast delivery (typically under a week), crazy cheap prices on discontinued designer yarns, reasonable shipping, plus an awesome sample program. You have to be a bit obsessive, though, because many of the yarns sell out in minutes. Sample program lets you preview upcoming closeouts (released on a schedule). And while you may not want to acknowledge you've pissed away $500 in yarn, they're nice enough to give you a $50 gift certificate kickback when you do. Plus good information, free patterns, and user swap meet area, too.

Flying Fingers (www.flyingfingers.com)
Wide assortment of luxury yarns, and absolutely fantastic, enormous pictures (a real plus when you can't feel the fibers), and cheap shipping. Pretty needles (Lantern Moon & Serendipity), lovely carved needle safes, and respectable sale prices.

Hello Yarn (www.helloyarn.com)
Handspun and hand-dyed beauties, everything gorgeous. Adrian (Hello Yarn) makes impossibly beautiful, lofty yarns in scrumptious colors, plus crazy corkscrew bobble yarns that you just want to eat (see the Strap Happy scarf in Chapter 4), and Sarah (Maisy Day Handspun) makes sproingy 2-plys that are a wonder to watch develop as you knit. Plus spinning supplies and kits, if you want to try your own hand, and wonderfully playful free patterns.

Herrschner's (www.herrschners.com)
Wide selection of both fancies & cheap yarns. Their sale site (www.yarnsale.com) has super discounts and lets you sort by brand, price, or discount percent. Their weekly yarn sale and occasional by-the-bag sales can be extraordinary. Plus wide notion and needle selection.

Jimmy Beans (www.jimmybeanswool.com)
Marvelous selection of fine yarns at standard prices, as well as respectable closeout sales. Quality needle selection, with a ton of hardwoods, cheap shipping, and speedy delivery. Plus pictures of their sweet dogs everywhere!

Knit Picks (www.knitpicks.com)
Lovely yarns and great prices. Especially cheap luxury alpacas and cashmere blends, with gorgeous colors. They also offer excellent discounts on books, some hard-to-find notions, and lots of free or cheap patterns. Cheap/free shipping.

Knitwerx (www.knitwerx.com)
Quick-shipping Canadian site. Great sorting (sort by fiber, brand, weight, price, etc.), excellent clearance section, plus everything comes all wrapped up in pretty green tissue, so it's like your birthday.

Knitter's Dream (www.knittersdream.com)
The online store of a LYS in PA. Fast, friendly service, and they carry the hard-to-find Mango Moon horn and bone needles, interchangeable bamboo sets, and clear Regia boots and clogs for you sock whores.

kpixie (www.kpixie.com)
Great indie shop with excellent assortment of one-of-a-kind yarns.

Smiley's (www.smileysyarns.com)
Lesser-known fancies and a wide selection of big brands, solid discount prices on current yarns and fantastic prices on discontinued yarns.

Stone Leaf Moon (www.stoneleafmoon.com)
Completely deranged, brilliant art yarn, every bit as wonderful as the pictures.

Webs (www.yarn.com)
Excellent selection of contemporary fine yarns, discounted 20% off $60 yarn purchase, 25% off $120. They're usually the cheapest option for current lines of high-end yarns, especially the ones you never see discounted. They have incredible closeout prices, and their own Valley Yarns line is pleasing and bargain priced. And I also have to prop them out for surprising color accuracy, a yummy array of needles, and knitting bags.

The Yarn Barn (www.yarnbarn-ks.com)
Online store for my LYS in Lawrence, Kansas. Standard prices on a wide assortment of yarns, plus bulk discounts, and a fine selection of magazine back issues.

Yarn Market (www.yarnmarket.com)
Wide array of better yarns, at standard prices. Cheap, speedy shipping and top-of-the-line customer service.

Everything Else

Your local or chain fabric store will usually carry bathing suit and lingerie notions, and all required fasteners.

Your local or chain hardware store will carry bulk (usually by-the-foot) rubber hose.

Corset Making Supplies (www.corsetmaking.com)
Fasteners, D-rings, garter clips, swivel hooks, etc. Smaller notions in the "Bra Making" section.

eBay (www.ebay.com)
It seems sort of obvious to mention ebay, but it's often the best place to get little odds and ends you can't find anywhere else, especially in small quantities. It's a little iffier than buying from a real store, but it's also often significantly cheaper.

Joann (www.joann.com)
Online home of brick-and-mortar craft chain offers frequent 40–50% off coupons, making it a great source for needles and notions, especially expensive needle sets, swifts, ball winders, etc. Excellent zoom feature gives you good close-up detail. Fasteners & lingerie notions are found under "sewing."

The Ribbon Jar (www.ribbonjar.com)
Lovely ribbons by the yard. All the basics, plus extra-fancy, unusual, and vintage ribbons to give your garment a special touch.

Tandy Leather (www.tandyleather.com)
Suede, leather, pleather, and plastic lacing (or buy a kit and make your own western belt!).

Abbreviations

beg	beginning
BO	bind off
CO	cast on
dpns	double-pointed needles
dec	decrease (if none is specified, use your favorite)
inc	increase (if none is specified, use your favorite)
k	knit
k2tog	knit two together. Knit 2 stitches together as if the were one (decrease).
M1	make one, invisible increase. With the left needle, lift the bar between the stitch you just knit and the next stitch from the front. Knit the lifted stitch tbl (increase).
p	purl
p2tog	purl two together. Purl 2 stitches together as if they were one (decrease) place marker.
psso	pass slipped stitch over. Draw the slipped stitch back over the stitch worked after it and drop it off the needle, sort of like binding off.
PU	pick up. Holding yarn as usual, insert right needle into finished st, YO and pull yarn through (essentially, knitting) to create a live stitch.
rnd	round (row, when knitting in the round)
RS	right side, the side that faces out, the public side
sl	slip. Slip stitch from left needle to right needle without working it. Always slip purlwise (with needle insterted from the right, as if to purl), unless indicated.
SM	slip marker
ssk	slip, slip, knit. Slip two stitches knitwise (inserting needle from left to right, as if you were about to knit the stitch), then insert your left needle into both stitches in front of right needle, then knit the two stitches together as one (decrease).
ssp	slip, slip, purl. Slip two stitches purlwise, then stick your left needle through both stitches behind the right needle, then purl both together as one (decrease).
st (s)	stitch(es).
tbl	through back loop. Knit through the side of the stitch in the back, away from you, instead of through the front side, the way you normally would. This twists the stitches, resulting in less stretch and a somewhat different appearance.
wrap	short-row wrap (see p. 134)
WS	wrong side, the body side of the work both from behind, and purl them together
yo	yarn over. Wrap yarn around right needle counter-clockwise, creating an extra stitch next row.
garter	knit all rows

Index